LEAP OF FAITH

THE STORY OF SCHNEIDER

LEAP OF FAITH

THE STORY OF SCHNEIDER

By Jim H. Smith

ESSEX PUBLISHING GROUP, INC.

Suggested retail price: $24.95

Printed and bound in the United States of America. No part of this publication may be reproduced or transmitted in any form or by any means, electronic or mechanical, including photocopying, recording or any information storage and retrieval system now known or to be invented, without permission in writing from Schneider, 3101 S. Packerland Drive, Green Bay, WI 54306-2545, except by a reviewer who wishes to quote brief passages in connection with a review for inclusion in a magazine, newspaper or broadcast.

Produced and published by Essex Publishing Group, Inc.,
St. Louis, Missouri.
www.essexink.com

Design by Clare Cunningham Graphic Design

Library of Congress Catalog Card Number: 2013945449

ISBN: 978-1-936713-03-5

First Printing: December 2014

Any trademarks in this book are property of their respective owners

Freightliner Cascadia® is a trademark of Daimler Trucks North America LLC

Bounty® is a trademark of The Procter & Gamble Company

All images courtesy of Schneider and its associates, except:

Page 16: ©Brad Whitsitt/Shutterstock
Page 77: ©Edward Hausner/The New York Times/Redux
Page 90: ©Press-Gazette Media

Table of Contents

CHAPTER ONE:

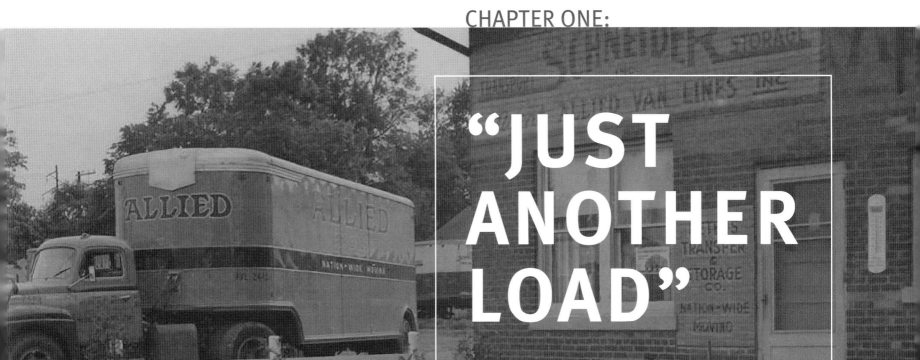

"JUST ANOTHER LOAD"

Schneider is little changed from its humble beginnings. It's still a family-centered company devoted to serving its customers well, treating people with respect, acting with integrity, delivering returns to reinvest in the business and making the roads as safe as they can possibly be.

The sun was just rising as drivers Julius Borley and Emil Elm arrived at the offices of Schneider Transport & Storage, Inc., in Green Bay, Wisconsin. They exchanged greetings with their dispatcher, Art Schmidt, a large man of few words. They punched a time clock, strode outside and clambered up into the cabs of twin International trucks the bright color of freshly dug carrots.

It was late summer, 1958, and Schneider had only recently acquired the trucks. They weren't new, but they were among the best in a fleet about which the word *junk* had often — and not altogether inaccurately — been tossed around. That morning, to the relief of Borley and Elm, the engines turned over easily and purred reliably, waiting to be engaged. After running the wipers a couple of times, the drivers pulled out, towing empty, 25-foot trailers. Their immediate destination: a Procter & Gamble (P&G) pulp mill in Green Bay almost directly across the Fox River from the Schneider facility.

Borley and Elm were both seasoned truckers in their thirties. Borley was an Army veteran. Honorably discharged from the service in 1946, he joined Schneider two years later, hauling whatever needed to be hauled

wherever customers needed it. A slightly built man, he put on muscle as he loaded and unloaded commodities such as beef quarters and 100-pound grain sacks. It was, he says, "bull work."

CHOSEN MEN

Among a cadre of 37 drivers in the 1940s, most of whose last names testified to Wisconsin's European immigrant heritage, Elm — who was generally known by his nickname, "Budd" — stood out; he was a Native American. But for a stint in the Navy, he'd lived his whole life within a few miles of where he worked. He was a driver's driver, a serious and soft-spoken man who showed up on time and always got the job done.

Borley and Elm hit it off soon after Borley joined the Schneider team, and by the summer of 1958, with Schneider's driver pool expanded to about 100 men, their safety records and devotion to the job had earned them seniority. It was why Al Schneider, the company's burly, cigar-chomping president, had chosen them for that morning's assignment.

Schneider is a $3.6 billion international business today, but as its headquarters, above, affirms, the company remains firmly rooted in Green Bay. That's where Al Schneider began his career as a taxicab driver and later launched the trucking company that bears the family name. Opposite, a Schneider truck from the 1950s.

ANOTHER STATE OF MIND

Borley and Elm drove their empty trucks eastward over the Fox River to P&G's Green Bay plant, where they were to pick up their cargo: two 45,000-pound loads of pressed lap — partially processed pulp compressed into sheets but not fully dried — stacked on pallets. The lap would ultimately be turned into napkins and tissue products at that plant, but first it needed to be refined in an intermediate step that at the time could only be done at another P&G facility in Cheboygan, Michigan. Schneider's job was to carry the lap to Cheboygan, wait for P&G to refine it there and then bring the load back to Green Bay.

What lay ahead of the drivers was a journey of nearly 300 miles, one-way. In trucks that under ideal circumstances could barely make 50 miles per hour while hauling a full load, it would take at least six hours — and these were by no means perfect conditions. Borley would recall years later that the trucks were inadequately powered for the task and that they were hardly traveling on modern interstate highways; these were two-lanes that had been dirt roads just a few years earlier. A little over an hour into the trip, they crossed the Menominee River and did something that no Schneider trucker had ever done before: they entered another state.

Trucking companies' capacity to grow at that time lay in their ability to wrest from the U.S. Interstate Commerce Commission authority to move products across state lines. In cutthroat competition with railroads (still the nation's dominant freight handler in the 1950s) and a growing cast of trucking companies, Schneider was willing to haul practically anything in order to obtain such traveling rights.

The fact that Schneider Transport could reliably make long hauls for a company as large and influential as Procter & Gamble was proof that it had the capacity to do such work for others. For 51-year-old Al Schneider, the

future was — quite literally — riding on Borley and Elm's delivery of that pulp.

The "Mighty Mac" bridge, opposite, between Michigan's upper and lower peninsulas was in many ways Schneider's gateway to the future, serving as the conduit to an important customer on the company's first interstate run in 1958. The men who made that run, left, were drivers Julius Borley, far left, and Emil "Budd" Elm, far right, center row.

THE CHEBOYGAN RUN

Beyond Marinette, the drivers continued northeast, with the shores of Green Bay and Big Bay de Noc to their right and the morning sun dancing on the water. Before long, they shed their jackets, rolled up their sleeves and cranked down the windows, grateful for a breeze in cabs that had no air-conditioning. When they reached Rapid River, Michigan, they turned due east along the southern shore of Michigan's Upper Peninsula. Soon they passed into the coniferous solitude of the Michigan National Forest, now called the Hiawatha National Forest.

It was early afternoon by the time the men reached St. Ignace. Long before they got there, they could see the distinctive profile of the "Mighty Mac," the immense, five-mile-long Mackinac Bridge, which had opened to fanfare only the previous November after three years of construction. When they drove across the windy sweep of the Straits of Mackinac, Al Schneider was waiting for them in Mackinaw City.

Schneider, who had driven to Michigan ahead of Borley and Elm so he could guide them to their

destination and add the personal touch to this all-important shipment, climbed into his car, and the truckers followed him down the final, 15-mile dogleg of their journey to Cheboygan. They delivered their cargo to the P&G plant on time and in good order. It took P&G eight hours to turn the 90,000 pounds of lap into enough eight-foot rolls of paper to fill the empty trailers. The loads were waiting when Borley and Elm showed up the next morning. Al Schneider had already departed, so the truckers set out on their own for the backhaul of what would become known as the "Cheboygan Run" — a lucrative round-trip for Schneider Transport.

"We didn't think it was anything special," recalls Borley. "We thought it was just another load."

In the annals of Schneider, that first trip to Cheboygan was comparable to the discovery of the Cumberland Gap in American history. The Cheboygan Run opened a door for Schneider that would enable the company to grow

in ways previously impossible. By the time Al Schneider's eldest son, Don, joined the company in 1961, a team of drivers was working around the clock, running eight loads per day between Green Bay and Cheboygan. An article in the *Detroit Free Press* declared Schneider to be by far the largest user of the Mackinac Bridge.

Today, Schneider is a $3.6 billion company that serves more than two-thirds of the *Fortune* 500. With operations in the United States, Canada, Mexico and China, it conducts business worldwide. From van truckload to bulk transport, intermodal to supply-chain management and logistics, Schneider offers the broadest array of services in the transportation and logistics industry. It has more than 17,000 employees (Schneider calls them "associates") and 2,200 independent contractors worldwide, more than 11,100 trucks and more than 48,000 trailers and containers on the road — a far cry from the one-man shop it began as back in 1935. Yet in a different sense, Schneider is little changed from its humble beginnings. Though it has grown in size and its ways of doing business have evolved with the times, it is still a company devoted to serving its customers well, treating people with respect, acting with integrity, delivering returns to reinvest in the business and making the roads as safe as they can possibly be.

On that summer morning in 1958, Schneider Transport & Storage was on the brink of greatness. Down the road, an extraordinary future awaited. But the company never could have made it to 1958 — let alone to Cheboygan — without the unbending perseverance of a man who barely had any money when he came to Green Bay seeking his fortune. In the spring of 1935, when America's industrial production was a full 25 percent lower than it had been in 1929 and hope was a hard thing to find, Al Schneider did something that became a defining characteristic of Schneider National: he took a leap of faith.

Amid radical changes in technology over 75 years, Schneider's values and culture have remained the same. The evolution in equipment is clear from outside three generations of Schneider trucks, but the most dramatic changes, which have distinguished Schneider from the pack, are inside the cab, where satellite-supported tracking and messaging capabilities have made operations faster, more precise and more efficient. Opposite, a driver loads unrefined petroleum at a well site. Schneider's bulk transport capabilities and supply-chain management expertise have positioned the company for continued growth in the bulk liquid chemical business.

The Schneider Way

There's the Schneider Way, or there's the highway. The Schneider Way is the fundamental approach to business that defines Schneider, and it has been defining the company since Al Schneider bought his first truck and went into business for himself during the dark days of the Great Depression.

Al's son, Don Schneider, spoke so often about the company and its fundamental values that those ideas took on gem-like weight and luster. CEO Chris Lofgren, who succeeded Don at the helm of the company, codified them in a written statement that articulates how Al kept his business going in spite of tough odds. "We exist to be a great and enduring enterprise, one that is privately held and creates value for our stakeholders," the Mission and Values statement called The Schneider Way reads. "We are a superior provider of services. Our pursuit of safety, excellence and innovation will not be outdone. We treat our customers, suppliers and associates with the utmost integrity without exception. We are committed to beneficial, lasting relationships as both an employer and a leader in the community. If our way was the 'easy way,' anyone could do it, but we're not just anyone. We are Schneider."

Al embodied those values, investing himself in the business as though his life depended on it, which it did. He worked long days. He hired good people and treated them fairly. He worked hard to attract customers in a highly competitive business.

And once he attracted a customer, he did everything in his power to make sure that customer remained happy with the service his company provided.

Based upon fundamental ideas that Al's son Don articulated, the four key values of Schneider's Mission and Core Values statement became the legs upon which the company stands tall and strong. They are impressed upon every associate from the moment he or she joins the company:

• **Safety first and always.** "We have a responsibility to our associates, customers and the community to operate safely. Nothing we do is worth harming ourselves or others."

• **Integrity in every action.** "We do what we say. We conduct our business with the highest ethical standards."

• **Respect for all.** "We treat everyone with dignity and respect. We embrace diversity of thought, experience and background."

• **Excellence in what we do.** "We do not stop until we've delivered a superior experience. We have a relentless passion for innovation and improvement."

These guiding principles are evident throughout the company's history. Without them, Schneider could not pursue its mission: "Safe, courteous, hustling associates delivering superior experiences that excite our customers." The values are indeed the company's stock and trade, every bit as important as Schneider's big, orange trucks and trailers that traverse North America's highways.

Military veterans and longtime Schneider drivers have had the honor of piloting the Ride of Pride, a Freightliner Cascadia truck specially decorated to salute America's men and women in the armed services. Left to right, Jay Hull, Randy Twine, Chuck Ceccacci, Richard Barczewski, Darrell Esson, Dave Carter and Bernard Johnson have all been behind the wheel of these special trucks.

CHAPTER TWO

TO GET
AN EDGE

Al Schneider spent 20 years as a member of the 432nd infantry division of the Wisconsin National Guard, rising to the rank of master sergeant. He valued his military experience highly, and much of what he learned in the Guard helped to shape him as a manager. Many years later, his sons also served in the Guard, and through the years, hundreds of Schneider associates would serve in the 432nd.

> The values Al carried with him into adulthood came from the church, the school of hard knocks and his parents. Those values he learned early on were like gold to him. He burnished them for a lifetime, and they grew to define him.

She was the very image of her time — a decidedly modern, young woman, dashing off for the evening, fashionably attired in a bright yellow duster and a veiled hat. Framed in the light from an automobile's headlamp, she adorned the cover of the Saturday, March 16, 1907, issue of *Harper's Weekly*. The popular magazine had built its circulation by brilliantly chronicling the shifting winds of American culture, and this issue focused on one of the fastest growing trends in the nation's history — the proliferation of automobiles. Articles covered automotive equipment, strategies for improving highways and ways to use cars in remote locations, as though all things were possible for those with a horseless carriage.

Most Americans, who at that time earned less than $1,000 a year, couldn't afford a motorcar that March. It would be another year and a half before Henry Ford's first affordable Model T would roll off his celebrated assembly line — and even then, it was a decidedly less convenient mode of transport than *Harper's Weekly* led its readers to believe.

Harper's Weekly wasn't selling cars, though. It was selling dreams — the kind of diversions that enabled ordinary, hard-working Americans like Jacob and Anna (Mannenbach) Schneider to escape from their humdrum lives for a few hours each week.

The Schneiders lived in Johnsburg, Wisconsin, a little town in eastern Fond du Lac County near the southern tip of Lake Winnebago. It was farm country densely populated by immigrant Germans. Acquiring an automobile was almost certainly the last thing on the Schneiders' minds that Saturday in 1907. They were people of decidedly modest means. Jacob Schneider eked out a living delivering groceries with a horse-drawn cart.

They also were welcoming their first child that day. It turned out to be a boy, and they gave him a fancy name: Aloysius. The name never fit him well, and he became known as "A. J." or "Al," the blunt little plug of a name the *Green Bay Press-Gazette* used in the story it published the morning after he died in Green Bay, just two weeks shy of his 76th birthday.

It's only 60 miles from Fond du Lac to Green Bay, but between those two places that formed the geographic bookends of his life, Al Schneider traveled far in more ways than one. He began by following in his father's footsteps.

THE DAWN OF TRUCKING

It was still a railroad world the year Al Schneider was born. What had been chartered as the Green Bay and Western in 1866 to ship lumber and produce had turned Green Bay into a growing transportation hub, connecting the agricultural upper Midwest with the industrial East.

Bins Transport had one wheel in the grave when Al Schneider bought it in 1938 and resurrected it. The Bins acquisition instantly transformed Al's owner-operator operation into a business with a fleet of trucks. That's Al, third from the right in the back row. Peter Bins, in the hat, is two men to the left of Al. Lawrence Bins and Harold Bins, Peter's nephews, are the last two men, respectively, on the far right in the bottom row.

Allied Van Lines had formed only recently when Al Schneider, who'd just purchased his first truck, signed on as an owner-operator for Allied's Green Bay agency, Jules Peters Transfer, in 1935. Al effectively launched his business with the purchase of that first truck, similar to the one shown here.

From 1900 to 1930, half a dozen regional railroads laid track to the city. Even in bustling Green Bay, automobiles were the exception. The first one seen in the area had arrived in 1900. It was a Duryea, a flimsy two-passenger contraption powered by a two-cylinder engine. The Springfield, Massachusetts, company that built it described it, accurately, as a "motor wagon."

Trucks — the conveyances that would carry Al Schneider down the road to his destiny — got off to an even later start than cars. The first was a pickup with a belt drive and two forward speeds that German automotive pioneer Gottlieb Daimler built 11 years before Al was born. Its motor delivered four horsepower, about a third of what a modern lawn tractor has.

Despite that inauspicious beginning, the growth of trucking was inevitable. By the time Al was three years old, there were about 10,000 trucks in the United States, almost all used as metropolitan delivery vehicles. They rolled on solid rubber tires that were durable but offered a spine-compressing ride. It would be 1920 before the introduction of pneumatic tires made it possible for trucks to go farther and faster — and for drivers to ride in something approaching comfort.

In 1917, the seeds of this growing industry took root in Wisconsin with the founding of the Oneida Motor Truck Company, which manufactured stake-sided trucks and, later, buses in Green Bay. Al Schneider was 10 years old and was one of those children who knew early on the course of his life. With the additions of two younger brothers — Bert and Clarence — and a younger sister, Esther, his family's meager resources had been stretched to the maximum.

With only three grades of public school behind him, Al terminated his formal education. Still a boy, he went to work, helping his father and picking up odd jobs. The values he carried with him into adulthood came from the church, the school of hard knocks and his parents

— a deliveryman father, who braved the worst weather Wisconsin could throw at him in order to provide for his family, and a housewife mother, whom Al's son Jim would remember as "a tough German woman, stout and mean." Those values he learned early on were like gold to Al. He burnished them for a lifetime, and they grew to define him.

GREEN BAY IN ASCENSION
The Roaring Twenties arrived in Green Bay like an early spring, with felicitous meteorological conditions conspiring to produce a bountiful growing season. In just 12 months, from 1919 to 1920, area bank deposits surged by $3 million. The city's Northern Paper Mill was the largest manufacturer of tissue in the nation, and more than 18 acres of new industrial space and 500 new homes were built.

Al Schneider brought neither formal education nor much of an estate to the task of finding a way to support himself and his young family in the darkest hours of the Great Depression. What he did have was a willingness to work hard and an unyielding determination not to fail.

Al and Agnes Schneider's sons Paul, left, and David were just children, but they were already bitten by the trucking bug when this photo was taken in the early 1940s. Both would eventually spend time working for their father, though both later left the company to pursue their own business interests.

The 1920s served as a tight, 10-year tunnel through which technology made a hyperkinetic leap forward, transforming America. Huge expanses of the nation were served, for the first time, with electric power that created vast new markets for a host of new household appliances such as clothes irons, toasters and vacuum cleaners. Radio made the world suddenly smaller, and roads improved significantly, making it smaller still as more people bought cars.

In Brown County, Wisconsin, at the beginning of the decade, there were maybe 2,000 motor vehicles and a scant 10 miles of paved highways. Five years later, practically every family in the county boasted a car, and by 1929 an average of more than 25,000 cars were being shipped across Lake Michigan to Green Bay every year. The city's economy was in ascension, and local businesses increasingly relied on trucks, more than 300,000 of which were by then registered for long-haul service in the United States.

"YOU'LL BE BACK"

Al Schneider was 22 in 1929, conditioned by years of tough physical labor. He'd learned all he could from his father. Still, instead of migrating north to sure opportunity in the city, he stayed in Fond du Lac. That's where he was on Thursday, October 24, when the stock market began its collapse. Over the next three-and-a-half years, the output of the industrial machine that had propelled America through the 1920s slumped by 50 percent. The income of the average American family shrank by a nearly equivalent amount. More than 5,500 banks, with total deposits in excess of $3 billion, tanked.

It was in the gloom of this economic chaos that 26-year-old Al Schneider made his move to Green

Bay. Like thousands of other Americans, driven off the family farm and out of small towns where jobs were as perishable as dust bowl crops, he went where he hoped work would be — where plenty of jobs had been only a few years earlier.

His sons recall a yellowed photograph that Al kept in their small home on Stuart Street in Green Bay when they were growing up. In the photo, taken sometime before he started his trucking business, Al stood in line with a number of other unemployed "joes," waiting hopefully for a day job, a few hours of employment that could make the difference between having dinner that night or going to bed hungry. All of the men in the photo wore workers' boots, bib overalls and gloves. Al alone sported a necktie. Son Jim Schneider recalls, "When we asked why he was wearing such an unlikely garment, he said, 'Work was so tight, I had to do something to get an edge.'"

"The local boys in Fond du Lac told him, 'You'll be back,'" says Al's son Paul. "They had seen plenty of others return with their tails tucked."

How little the local boys knew Al. When he left for Green Bay, he packed a steely determination and an unflinching work ethic. He was damned if he would fail. In Green Bay, he tackled his job search with a resourcefulness that would become one of the hallmarks of his career. By that point, 90 percent of Brown County's 1,300 miles of roads were classified as "all-weather," and more than 200 were paved, 64 in Green Bay. If there was one thing Al Schneider knew how to do, it was drive; and before long he was behind the wheel of a taxicab, where he learned the lay of the land.

Gregarious by nature, he met people and made friends. Soon he transitioned from taxi to truck, driving for various Green Bay companies. By 1934, there was no possibility he would be mistaken for some down-at-the-heels bumpkin from the sticks shuffling around town with hat in hand. He'd established himself as a dependable, hard-working driver. He was digging in.

When Al returned to Fond du Lac that year, it was to marry the girl he'd left behind. Her name was Agnes Halfmann, and they wed on June 5, 1934, at St. Peter Church in Johnsburg. Like her husband, Agnes had dropped out of school early — though her eight years of common school trumped Al's three — after her father, Joseph Halfmann, a railroad mail sorter, was seriously injured and lost his job. One of nine kids raised in a tiny family homestead with a dirt floor, she found work in the summer homes of wealthy people.

Clarence Schneider, like his older brother, was bent upon becoming a trucker. He married Agnes' sister and followed Al to Green Bay. Brother Bert then left Fond du Lac and headed to Milwaukee, where he remained in trucking for many years before relocating to Columbus, Ohio, to pursue a career in general commodity sales.

While the Schneider brothers were bitten by the transportation bug, their sister, Esther, was immune. She followed her dreams to the West Coast and married a man who earned a living taking far fewer risks than her brothers. He was a stuntman in the movies.

AL SADDLES UP

At some point in the history of every great company, the founder or founders stand upon a cliff where they have a choice: turn back or take the plunge. Al Schneider reached that brink in March 1935. The action he took may have been precipitated by the fact that Agnes was pregnant with their first child, or he may have done it simply because, taking stock of his life on his 28th birthday, he was determined that he would not go another year without seizing the wheel of his destiny. Whatever his motives, Al sold his car, a 1932 Plymouth, and bought his first truck with the proceeds. It was a used, two-and-a-half-ton International B model — no

great shakes as trucks go — but it was Al's pony, and he would ride it for the next three years in the service of several companies.

While the Depression lingered on, it was clear that the nation could not rebound without transportation. To put unemployed workers back on the job, manufacturing needed to resume, and consumers needed to start buying goods again. Al reasoned it would take both trains and trucks to move those goods.

The industry in which he began his career was a helter-skelter affair. Many drivers at the time were, like Al, owner-operators. Displaced from other work by the Depression, they had taken to the roads to survive. This may have given rise to the romantic, cowboy notion of the American trucker — a tough independent carving out his own destiny — but driving trucks was hardly a life of stability or certain success.

Al and Agnes Schneider posed with all of their children for this family portrait, which accompanied their Christmas cards in 1956. Don Schneider stands in the center of the back row, flanked by his brothers Paul, left, and David. Left to right, between Agnes and Al, are Kathleen, Jim and John.

Striving for Zero

When Don Osterberg, senior vice president of safety, security and driver training for Schneider, spoke at the American Trucking Associations Management Conference in Las Vegas in the fall of 2009, he told his audience that sleep apnea was a significantly under-diagnosed disorder, "grossly underreported" in accidents. Not testing drivers and requiring those with the disorder to obtain treatment was threatening highway safety and exposing transportation fleets to both liability and greater health care expense.

Sleep apnea — a disorder in which a person experiences repeated abnormal pauses in breathing during sleep — may seem a strange concern for the head of safety and security at a major transportation company. However, the disorder disrupts the sleep of those who suffer from it, often leaving them fatigued when they're awake. This is not merely an issue of productivity; sleep apnea can make truck drivers unsafe behind the wheel.

Acknowledging that the industry was taking many steps to improve highway safety, Osterberg cautioned, "We need to be careful what we celebrate. Fourteen people will be killed in truck-related crashes today, and 14 will die tomorrow. That is too many. We need to strive for that to be zero." It was a typical position for Osterberg, who less than a year later was awarded the first-ever Distinguished Safety Leadership Award by the Truck Safety Coalition, a partnership between Citizens for Reliable and Safe Highways (CRASH) and Parents Against Tired Truckers (PATT).

"Don has always pushed the industry envelope when it comes to safety on our nation's highways," said Jeff Burns, a board member of both organizations and the National Transportation Counsel for the Truck Safety Coalition. "He doesn't just talk about truck safety. He pursues it with a vengeance and follows up with persistent reassessment and improvement."

Schneider has always had a commitment to safety — one of the company's core values. But under the leadership of Osterberg, who joined Schneider in October 2000, Schneider's preventable crash rate has declined by 30 percent, fatigue-related crashes have been cut by 27 percent and the fatal crash rate has been reduced by nearly 60 percent.

Relying on careful analysis of driver-related data, Osterberg and his team have been able to identify risk-prone drivers with increasing reliability, intervening before accidents become inevitable. With increasingly sophisticated training programs, improved equipment and technology such as simulators that approximate the experience of driving a big rig, Osterberg and his team are working to make Schneider the safest transportation company on the planet.

Regardless of their experience, no one gets to drive for Schneider without spending time at the wheel of one of the company's simulators — essential tools in Schneider's goal to become the world's safest transportation company. Instructors use the simulators to test drivers' skills and to challenge them with a variety of road hazards and weather conditions.

Workers relax in the locker room at Olson Transportation, the company for which Al Schneider drove just before he leased his trucks to Bins Transport.

NATIONAL REGULATION OF TRUCKING

Railroads still dominated freight hauling at the time Al got into the business, and they gobbled up the choicest accounts. Competition was fierce among truckers, but with the industry financially weak, service tended to be unreliable; shippers often had no assurance of either delivery schedules or transportation costs. Something had to change if the industry was to grow. Individual states tried to solve the problem first, establishing regulations to ensure that trucking companies operated uniformly. It was a good idea, but it failed to take into consideration that different states might have conflicting regulations. So, in the summer of 1935, after Al bought his first truck, Congress stepped in and passed the Motor Carrier Act, amending the Interstate Commerce Act of 1887 and imposing upon trucking companies the same kind of national regulations that already existed for railroads.

The act divided the industry into two classifications — private and for-hire carriage — and defined nation-wide standards for each. Private fleets were those owned by companies whose principal business was not transportation. For-hire companies carried freight belonging to others. The for-hire category was further divided into three distinct classifications: common carriers, which provided service to the general public; contract carriers, which were essentially in-house carriers; and exempt carriers, which handled commodities such as agricultural goods. In order to haul goods across state lines, carriers of all types first had to obtain authority from the Interstate Commerce Commission (ICC). Authorities were very limited, hard to come by and required in essence that every shipper, every commodity and every first load be approved by the ICC. Carriers were forbidden from showing up at a shipper's door and offering to haul their freight. Doing so was considered criminal.

A carrier had to demonstrate to the commission's satisfaction that its service was in the public's best interest. Even though favorable shipping costs were in the public's best interest, cost could not be used as evidence in pursuit of authority.

Public interest was not a matter of great concern to owner-operator Al Schneider when he began driving in 1935 for Jules Peters Transfer, an agency of the recently formed Allied Van Lines. It was a good job by the standards of the time. Peters and its parent company obtained the ICC authorities; Al simply drove. A round-trip from Green Bay to Minneapolis took some 16 hours in a truck like Al's International, which lumbered along at 38 miles per hour; but the work was steady, and Al was especially grateful for a predictable paycheck when his first son, Donald, was born on October 19, 1935. Al and Agnes would go on to have six children; Don was followed by David in 1937, Paul in 1939, Jim in 1946, John in 1948 and Kathleen in 1951.

Al Schneider was determined to be his own boss, and the one-year stint with Peters Transfer was the start of three years during which he was biding his time, working for others while looking for the right opportunity to strike out on his own. From Peters, he went to the Bur Wholesale Company, where he hauled beer from Milwaukee. A single load in his 20-foot trailer put about $30 in Al's pocket. By 1938, he had scraped together enough cash to purchase a second truck, and he was calling his young company A. J. Schneider and Sons.

He was driving for Olson Transportation then, but early in 1938 he leased his trucks to a Green Bay moving and storage operation called Bins, which was struggling financially. Al, soon named general manager, hoped he could turn it around. Instead, Bins declared bankruptcy, and for the first time in five years, Al was jobless. The prospect of trying to make it as an owner-operator no longer appealed to him. He was 31, and it was time to make his stand. In June, he used Agnes's dowry to buy

Olson Transportation was one of several Green Bay trucking companies for which Al drove before he banked on Bins, a gamble that came close to failing but ultimately turned into a success story that continues to this day. Above is Olson's Green Bay office; at left, its multi-hued fleet.

In 1944, Al Schneider bought Peters Transfer, the Allied Van Lines operation for which he'd driven in the mid-1930s, and soon consolidated his expanding business in this building at 817 McDonald Street in Green Bay. It would serve as the company's headquarters for nearly three decades. Al rebranded the trucks, opposite, with the Schneider name after purchasing Bins Transport in 1938, though they still displayed the Bins name.

the greatly depreciated Bins operation. On June 6, 1938, he incorporated it as Schneider Transport & Storage, Inc. Employees of the company and nearly everyone with whom the company did business soon shortened that to just Schneider Transport.

HUMBLE BEGINNINGS

When Al Schneider bought Bins, he got a fleet of poorly maintained blue-and-white trucks, ICC authority to haul beer from Milwaukee, nine drivers who were grateful that Al had salvaged their jobs and a small side business storing household goods. In Green Bay, the majority of work to be done was local cartage and some interstate trucking. Those who landed jobs tended to hold on to them. If they survived until the economy rebounded, they expected to have a fighting chance.

Since he had no money to buy new trucks, Al employed mechanics to keep his jerry-rigged fleet on

the road. Paul Schneider remembers that, even as late as when he was in high school, his friends used to make fun of the company's equipment. "The story around town was that, if a truck was broken down by the side of the road, it must be a Schneider truck," says Paul. It didn't help that Schneider maintained a junkyard near the Fox River, where Al's mechanics picked the bones of derelict trucks for parts that could be recycled to keep other vehicles on the road. In Al Schneider's world, thriftiness was next to godliness.

He moved Schneider Transport & Storage in 1938 to Jackson Street in Green Bay, where it operated out of the former stable of a local brewery that had been a casualty of Prohibition. For the next several years, the company remained in those humble quarters. Business gradually improved, but it would be a long time before Al felt like he could relax.

In 1944, he closed his independent storage business and made two important moves: First, he purchased Peters Transfer, the Allied Van Lines agency for which he had driven; the acquisition made the operation larger and more secure. The second big move was out of the former brewery and into a larger space at 817 McDonald Street in Green Bay. Nearby, in a little house that had been eclipsed by industrial space and corralled by railroad tracks, he set up his Allied operation. In an adjacent warehouse, he stored furniture for Allied.

As buildings go, the new office was anything but sophisticated. The upstairs — where some employees labored beneath low-hanging rafters upon which they periodically whacked their heads when they stood up — was referred to as the "hay mow." It hadn't changed much by the time Richard "Dick" Schluttenhofer joined the company nearly three decades later. He generously recalls it as "rustic." Nevertheless, it was where the hardscrabble business found its footing and began to take on the appearance of a substantial trucking operation.

SCHNEIDER TRANSPORT & STORAGE INC.
MOVING · PACKING · SHIPPING · STORAGE · HEAVY HAULING

TRANSPORT SCHNEIDER STORAGE
INC.

232
SCHNEIDER
GREEN BAY WIS.

GREEN BAY A. 516   MANITOWOC 5692

PACKING · CRATING · SHIPPING · STORING · HEAVY HAULING

TRUCK TERMINAL   DISTRIBUTION   232

LOCAL & LONG DISTANCE
MOVING

CHAPTER THREE

OVER HIS HEAD FROM THE BEGINNING

Transformed from lone-wolf driver to head of an expanding trucking empire, Al Schneider was about 20 years into his career when he convened most of his workforce for this photo in 1958. Al is fourth from the right in the first row; his brother Clarence is on the far right in the same row. The photo shows many veteran Schneider drivers, including Roger Klein, third from the left in the first row; "Budd" Elm and Julius Borley, standing, sixth and eighth, respectively, from the right in the third row; and Merlin Lardinois, 14th from the right in the same row.

Between 1945 and 1980, 75 percent of federal funds for transportation were spent on highways. A huge amount went into construction of the Interstate Highway System, officially known as the Dwight D. Eisenhower National System of Interstate and Defense Highways. The largest public works project in history, it cost more than $400 billion, and it literally paved the way for trucking's future.

Al Schneider discovered that running a company was a decidedly different matter from driving his own truck. The skill set that made him a good, reliable driver was barely adequate to the task of managing a fleet, even a small one. But for an uncompromising work ethic and a bullheaded determination, he might have failed. His sons say Al was motivated by fear: everything he and Agnes had was tied up in the business.

"My dad was in over his head in this business from the beginning," declares Paul Schneider, "but he kept going and he learned as he went. The business was all-consuming." David Schneider agrees. "He never gave up. He was very determined, always ready to do something new."

Al's primary task was acquiring customers. Trucking companies that wished to obtain ICC authority for routes had to correctly answer three questions: Did what the company proposed to offer "serve a useful public purpose, responsive to a public demand or need?" Could companies that already existed deliver the service? Was the applicant capable of providing the service "without endangering or impairing the operations of existing [companies]?"

The ICC requirements restricted competition between trucking companies and railroads, as well as between common and contract carriers within the trucking industry; but they also made it next to impossible for new companies to enter the industry. Without at least one authority, a trucking company couldn't operate, and it couldn't grow without continually obtaining additional authorities. Consequently, it was rare for trucking companies to have sales staff. What trucking companies really needed were lawyers. In fact, argues Thomas Vandenberg, Schneider National's longtime general counsel, lawyers were the de facto salespeople for many trucking firms in those days.

By the 1940s, Schneider Transport & Storage had become large and logistically complex enough to require forklift drivers in its warehousing operation.

In order to obtain ICC authority for routes, companies had to make their appeals in hearings that were in many respects like trials. Witnesses were paraded in to back the company's claim. Often those witnesses were representatives of customers with which the trucking firm was already doing business. They would support the carrier's claims that the service was needed, that the public was encumbered for its lack and that the carrier had proven its capacity to provide reliable service safely. But they resented being pressed into service. Time spent testifying was time spent away from their businesses. Hearings could drag on for days, and the only reason a witness would carry a trucking company's banner was because he wanted to stay on the good side of the firm upon which he depended to move his own products. The company that ventured before the ICC without an attorney schooled in transportation law risked finding itself out of business. So Al, though not wealthy, got comfortable with lawyers right away.

There was another way a trucking company could obtain authorities: buy a company that already had them. Al had acquired authorities to haul beer and milk when he bought Bins Moving and Storage; and when he bought Peters Transfer, the Allied Van Lines' moving and storage authorities came with it. They were enough to build on.

ROOTS IN BEER AND PAPER

Beer making is a storied industry with deep roots in Wisconsin. Milwaukee had so many breweries, it became known as the "beer capital of the world." To Green Bay distributors Beer Inc. and Bur Wholesale, Schneider drivers trucked amber oceans of Schlitz, Pabst, Blatz and Miller from Milwaukee and Old Style Lager from LaCrosse, Wisconsin.

Paper was also a big source of revenue for Schneider. Green Bay was Wisconsin's paper capital. When Al launched his enterprise, the city was home to such prominent paper-products manufacturers as Procter & Gamble; Charmin (which P&G later purchased); Fort Howard; Northern; Nicolet, which made papers used for candy, cheese wrappers and potato chip bags; and Bay West, a division of Mosinee Paper that produced hand wipes, windshield-wiper cloths for service stations and a variety of other finished paper products.

Al was fortunate — and wise — to cultivate an enduring friendship with Arnold Long, the general manager of Bay West. Avid anglers and hunters, the men spent countless hours together tromping through the woods of northern Wisconsin in search of fish and game.

"Arnold helped my father make contacts with other people in the paper industry," says Paul Schneider. "He knew everyone, and he helped Dad acquire paper-hauling authority and get connected."

Before long, Schneider was hauling for all of the paper companies.

By the 1950s, when some 30 trucking companies vied for business in Green Bay, Charmin — which had three Green Bay plants — kept many Schneider drivers busy full time. Moreover, Al rented warehouse space from the McDonald Lumber Company at Bay Beach, where he stored Charmin products until they were ready to be loaded onto railroad boxcars.

STRONG-ARM TACTICS

As if he didn't have enough of a challenge in obtaining authorities, Al Schneider soon found himself grappling with another foe. His company was only a few years old when, one day, a stone-faced representative of the International Brotherhood of Teamsters (IBT) paid him a visit. The union had a proposition for Schneider: become a union shop or be shut down.

Between 1935 and 1941, the Teamsters' membership exploded by nearly 400 percent. The union was becoming one of the nation's most powerful labor organizations and was intent on getting bigger. By the time Al had acquired Bins, the Teamsters were aggressively organizing trucking companies all over the Midwest, often relying on "strong-arm tactics," says former Schneider associate Don Jauquet in his personal memoir of the company's labor issues, *A History of the Significant Labor Relations Events at Schneider Transport, Inc. and Schneider National, Inc.: 1935–2008.* "[They] approached Transport, dropped the contract on the desk and indicated that the choice was to sign it or be shut down," Jauquet wrote. That was how Schneider Transport became a union shop, and the

Teamsters' ultimatum set the tone for the company's interactions with the union for years.

TOUCH-AND-GO FINANCIALS

Schneider Transport & Storage began its second decade in 1948 with $2,144 in cash, about a thousand dollars more than it had at the beginning of 1947. It had an impressive $82,542 tied up in assets, the value of which was reduced by more than $33,000 for depreciation and amortization. There were $5,778 in receivables, but they were far more than offset by liabilities, including nearly $37,000 in accounts payable.

The beer and paper contracts notwithstanding, business was always a tenuous proposition. Some weeks, it was ample; other weeks, thin. Some customers would engage Schneider drivers for a short time and then have no more work for weeks. The unpredictability of cash flow was nerve-wracking. Al and former schoolteacher Dorothy Tomachek — who was by then handling billings, payroll and, with Marie Ahearn, customer service for the company — became adept at stretching a dollar.

Hard work was the norm, and Al set the bar high, with countless days that started before daybreak and

After purchasing Jules Peters Transfer, the Green Bay agency for Allied Van Lines, Al Schneider retained Peters' Phoebe Street address, as this newspaper ad from 1946 shows, until he could consolidate the Allied business into the company's other operations on McDonald Street. The cargo in the truck on the opposite page might have been beer, paper pulp or even cucumbers or pickles transported for one of Green Bay's canneries. Schneider truckers hauled all kinds of commodities, from the conventional to the bizarre. If it wasn't illegal and money could be made moving it from one place to another, Al Schneider seldom turned business down.

yawned on deep into the evening. He never asked his employees to do something he wasn't prepared to do himself, and the sun rarely rose on a day, including Sundays, when he didn't at least check in at McDonald Street. Every day, he spent time talking with all of his mechanics, who, unlike his drivers, never joined the Teamsters. Al forestalled discontent in the shop by compensating the mechanics at the same hourly rates that the union negotiated for the drivers. He knew how much he depended on the mechanics to keep his trucks on the road and how badly they could cripple his business if they went on strike.

"My dad didn't get ahead by taking advantage of anyone," says Jim Schneider. "When things were tough and cash was tight, the employees were always paid first. Dad took compensation last, if there was enough."

John Schneider recalls, "One evening, when we were kids, [Al] was with us at home, and he showed us this check made out to him in the amount of 23 cents. We asked him what it was for, and he told us it was one week's paycheck. 'This is what I took home after I paid everybody,' he said."

Fridays were paydays, and many of the drivers, thirsty at the end of a long week, cashed their checks at Mike Tilkens Tavern, a gritty, blue-collar watering hole near Schneider's McDonald Street facility. Ask any of Schneider's older associates, and they'll tell you Al Schneider never missed a payroll. "When things were tight, he would call Mike Tilkens and ask him to hold the checks until Monday to make sure there was enough money to cover the checks," says Jim Schneider. Just as he never let his employees down, neither did Al betray Tilkens' trust. "Come Monday, the checks were always good," says long-time associate Mary Gronnert, Don Schneider's administrative assistant for 30-plus years.

Schneider was willing to haul just about anything. Old timers recall pulling trailers loaded with such freight

as stinking animal hides, 55-gallon drums filled with formaldehyde-pickled baby sharks, and a resinous byproduct of pulp processing called lignin pitch. Using tankers with attachments, Schneider truckers spread the pitch on Wisconsin dirt roads throughout the summer months to compact the dirt and keep dust down. That provided steady work for Schneider every year until the early 1970s.

TRUCKING (AND TEAMSTERS) ON THE RISE

Three important trends reshaped the trucking industry and the fabric of American society in the years after World War II. For starters, there was the breakneck migration of people from cities to suburbs. Across the country, a generation of young Americans, with the economic depression and war behind them, discovered that the American dream meant they could own a piece of land in the suburbs, away from the crush of cities where their parents, often immigrants, had lived in congested and sometimes squalid tenements. The flight to suburbia was accompanied by the rapid expansion of

Although nearly all of Schneider's trailers in the 1940s and '50s were vans, the company also had flatbed trailers, as seen at the McDonald Street facility, left. Sides of beef, above, from a meatpacking plant were among the many types of cargo the young company carried in the early days.

Pumpkin Trucks

The color has several names: blaze orange, vivid orange or — as any Schneider truck driver will tell you — Omaha orange. It's the bright, hard-to-miss shade that distinguishes most of Schneider's trucks and all of its trailers from other vehicles on the road.

Whatever its name, orange hasn't always been Schneider's official color. For the first six years of the company's existence, most Schneider trucks were blue and white, the color Al Schneider inherited when he bought Bins Transport in the summer of 1938. It wasn't until 1944, when Schneider became an agent for Allied Van Lines, that Allied required all Schneider vehicles to sport the distinctive orange that Allied vehicles were already using.

There was more to the request than cosmetics or branding. Yet another name for Omaha orange — perhaps the one known most widely outside the United States — is safety orange. It's such a striking shade that it stands in contrast to nearly all natural surroundings. Small wonder that it's the color of choice for high-visibility clothing (such as hunter's jackets, vests and hats) and safety equipment used in connection with highway construction, such as cones, barrels and stanchions.

For Don Schneider, safety was always the most important reason for having a bright orange fleet. He would often assert that the color was chosen because it's the easiest to spot on the road and thus the safest. Don's point was well taken. His father

understood how the color made his equipment and his drivers safer. Since the color quickly became synonymous with the company, it has been a key element of Schneider's brand since that time —

underscoring the company's commitment to safety, the first of Schneider National's core values.

Schneider became identified with the color almost as soon as the fleet was repainted. Lots in

and around Green Bay where Schneider vehicles were parked became known as "pumpkin patches." When bright orange cones and barrels became the norm at construction sites, truckers nationwide took to calling them "Schneider eggs," and a couple generations of American kids have reportedly played the "Schneider Game," trying to be the first to spot the colorful trucks on long family road trips.

Schneider trucks are often called "pumpkin trucks," its lots "pumpkin patches."

Having survived the hardscrabble years, Schneider was a viable entity by the time nearly 40 of Al Schneider's drivers posed for this photo at McDonald Street in the late 1940s. Al, in coat and tie, stands to their left.

highways that enabled workers to commute to their jobs back in the cities. Simultaneously, many of those jobs came to the workers as companies established offices in or relocated altogether to new population centers in what not long before had been farmland.

All of this set the stage for a profound change in transportation patterns. In the 1800s and the first half of the 1900s, the majority of American businesses had been concentrated in cities, where it was easy for railroads to serve them. As companies moved out, railroads, lacking spurs to service suburban facilities, found it harder to offer end-to-end service. It was a weakness that trucking companies eagerly exploited. They also took advantage of the many railroad strikes in the mid-1900s during which truckers were granted emergency authority to move freight. When customers discovered how efficient the truckers were, they often were unwilling to resume shipping by rail.

In 1950, nearly 65 percent of the nation's goods traveled by rail; less than 30 percent by trucks. Railroads would never have it so good again. By the early 1970s, the imbalance shifted. Aided by construction of the Interstate Highway System, trucks became the nation's dominant freight transporter. Rail's share had slipped to 35 percent by 1978.

Also in ascension were the unions. In 1946, an estimated five million Americans took part in protracted labor strikes. The following June, Congress passed the Labor-Management Relations Act, often referred to as the Taft-Hartley Act. The law prohibited wildcat strikes, secondary boycotts and closed shops. Unions could no longer donate to the campaigns of politicians running for federal offices.

The Teamsters, in turn, found ways to consolidate immense fiscal power through funds purportedly created to serve their members. In 1950, for example, the union established the Central States Health and Welfare Fund,

covering the entire Midwest. Five years later, the Central States Pension Fund was introduced. Unionized trucking companies throughout the region, like Schneider, were compelled to participate.

GROWING UP IN A GROWING BUSINESS

As they neared adolescence, each of Al Schneider's sons got an opportunity to work in the business, whether he wanted to or not. No mollycoddler, Al was determined that his boys would make something of themselves, whether it was with Schneider Transport or in some other profession. Rather than entering the family business, Al's daughter, Kathleen, moved to the East Coast and established her career there.

Paul Schneider recalls that his father "had high expectations, and if we didn't tow the mark, he was a hard man. He was teaching us how to be resilient; and if he was tough, he also had a good heart. He taught us to be honest, strong and fair."

Recalls John, "Dad would pay me a quarter an hour. When I was pretty young, I'd walk out to the warehouse, two or three miles from our house, and sweep up or clean up between the railroad tracks."

All of the Schneider boys eventually worked in the McDonald Street yard, fueling trucks. They learned to drive the tractors, each of which seemed to have a unique personality. Learning to drive them was a process that called for — or quickly gave one — a thick skin. Jim Schneider recalls the day his father took him to the yard for the first time and had one of the drivers "teach" him to drive. "He showed me where the shifting lever was and where the pedals were, and that was about it," says Jim. "After that, I was on my own." Jim, whose feet barely reached the pedals, spent an embarrassing afternoon teaching himself to drive the truck. He turned it into a personal challenge, though, and mastered the process. Once he knew how to drive the trucks, he began parking

Al's son Paul, above, had a long career with Schneider. He joined the company in 1962 as operations manager and stayed until 1986, spending his last 18 years as head of Schneider Tank Lines, a successful division he forged after the acquisition of the former Kampo Transit.

them in a more orderly fashion, enhancing operations.

In time, most of the Schneider boys also served in the 432nd infantry division of the Wisconsin National Guard, which their father had joined. Al remained in the Guard for 20 years, rising to the rank of master sergeant. He brought a lot of what he learned in the Guard about effective leadership to his business.

By the time Don and Dave Schneider were in high school, they were working for their father steadily as mechanic's helpers and truck drivers. After Dave graduated, he stayed with the company, but Al often employed him like a bench player, throwing him into service whenever a trucker was unavailable or dispatching him to acquire parts or retrieve a disabled truck. By his mid-20s, Dave felt underutilized.

Don, meanwhile, tucked his money away to pay for an education at St. Norbert College, a small, Catholic liberal arts school in nearby De Pere, Wisconsin. Neither he nor his father had any idea at the time what an investment Al was making in the future of his business with every dollar he paid Don.

By then, Don was already deeply invested in his father's company, says Patricia "Pat" O'Brien Schneider, the girl he met one afternoon in 1952 when he visited her home to help one of her brothers with a school project. Don was 17 and Pat was 15, and he soon invited her to a dance. Within a year, they were going steady.

She could tell right away that her new beau was an ambitious young man. "Every time we went to a movie," she recalls, "we ended up driving to the company at the end of the evening to make sure everything was okay, even if we were on a double date. Don was always thinking about the business."

On June 15, 1957, two weeks after Don graduated from college, he and Pat were married. He had enlisted in the Army, and before shipping out that September for a 13-month tour of duty in South Korea, he spent the

summer driving trucks for his father and padding his nest egg.

When he returned home from Korea, he was intent upon getting more education. The end of the 1950s found Don and Pat in Philadelphia, where he was enrolled at the University of Pennsylvania's prestigious Wharton School of Business, pursuing a master's degree with the same ferocity he would soon focus upon developing the family business.

LEAPING FORWARD

Between 1945 and 1980, 75 percent of federal funds for transportation were spent on highways. A huge amount went into construction of the Interstate Highway System, officially known as the Dwight D. Eisenhower National System of Interstate and Defense Highways. The largest public works project in history, it cost more than $400 billion, and it literally paved the way for trucking's future.

Al's connections with the Wisconsin paper industry continued to pay off; by the 1950s, he had added as customers the Cornell Paper Company, based in Cornell, Wisconsin, and Diana Manufacturing, which produced paper products for hospitals and other health care facilities. Diana was more than just a good customer. In the 1960s, as Schneider Transport grew, leaders of Diana supported Al as he acquired authority to haul paper products and chemicals used in paper manufacture to 26 states. Schneider also hauled meat for several companies and cheese for the Green Bay–based Pauly Cheese.

In 1960, regulations changed, and trucking companies could use 40-foot trailers, a full 15 feet longer than the industry standard to that point, prompting Al to buy four new International trucks. They were the first brand-new vehicles the company had acquired in its 22 years of existence. Says Paul Schneider: "I think that's when Dad actually felt like a success for the first time."

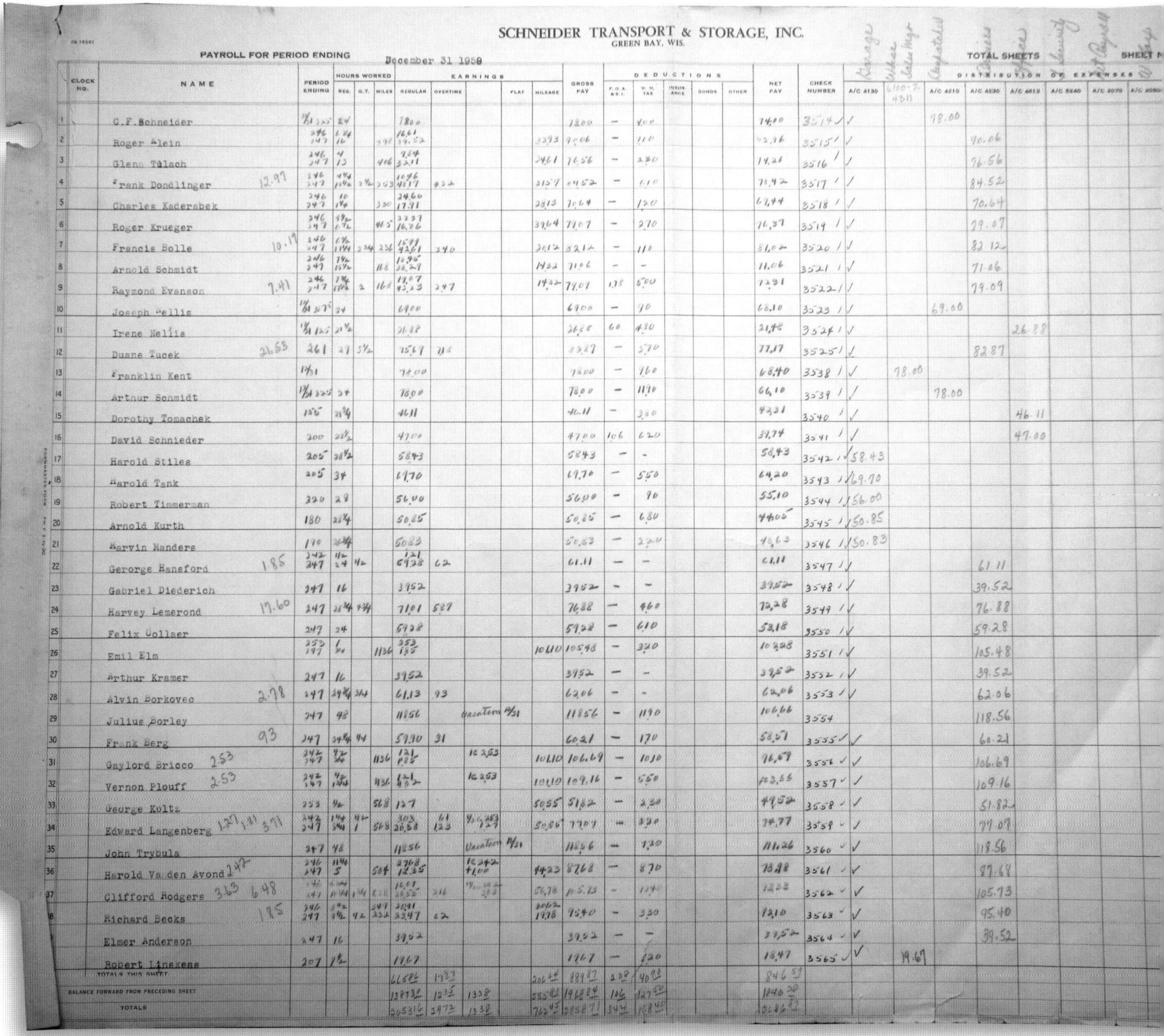

SCHNEIDER TRANSPORT & STORAGE, INC.
GREEN BAY, WIS.

PAYROLL FOR PERIOD ENDING December 31 1958

TOTAL SHEETS   SHEET N

CLOCK NO.	NAME	PERIOD ENDING	REG.	O.T.	MILES	REGULAR	OVERTIME	FLAT	MILEAGE	GROSS PAY	F.O.A.B.&I.	W.H. TAX	INSUR-ANCE	BONDS	OTHER	NET PAY	CHECK NUMBER	A/C 4130	A/C 6100-2 4311	A/C 4210	A/C 4230	A/C 4413	A/C 5240	A/C 2079	A/C
1	C.F. Schneider	12/31 245	24			7800				7800	—	400				74.00	3514	✓			78.00				
2	Roger Klein	246 247	144 12		278	1661 39.52			2393	9006	—	110				45.96	3515	✓			90.06				
3	Glenn Tilach	246 247	13		406	984 32.11			2461	7056	—	230				74.26	3516	✓			76.56				
4	Frank Dondlinger	246 247	44½ 19¼	3½	253	1096 45.19	422		2159	8452	—	110				73.42	3517	✓			84.52				
5	Charles Kaderabek	246 247	10 17½		330	2460 17.91			2813	7664	—	120				69.44	3518	✓			70.64				
6	Roger Krueger	246 247	9½		415	2237 16.86			3964	7907	—	270				76.37	3519	✓			79.07				
7	Francis Bolle	246 247	6½ 19¼	234	236	1599 43.61	340		2012	8212	—	110				81.02	3520	✓			82.12				
8	Arnold Schmidt	246 247	7½ 15½		116	1495 50.29			1432	7106	—	—				71.06	3521	✓			71.06				
9	Raymond Evanson	246 247	1½ 19¾	2	160	1107 45.13	247		1422	7907	1.38	500				72.31	3522	✓			79.09				
10	Joseph Sellis	12/31 243	24			6900				6900		90				68.10	3523	✓		69.00					
11	Irene Nellis	12/31 125	21¼			2688				2688	60	430				21.98	3524	✓						26.88	
12	Duane Tucek	261	27	5½		7569	216			8287	—	570				77.17	3525	✓			82.87				
13	Franklin Kent	12/31				7800				7800	—	160				68.40	3538	✓	78.00						
14	Arthur Schmidt	12/31 320	24			7800				7800	—	1190				66.10	3539	✓		78.00					
15	Dorothy Tomachek	155	21¾			4611				4611		230				43.31	3540	✓					46.11		
16	David Schneider	200	28½			4700				4700	106	620				39.74	3541	✓					47.00		
17	Harold Stiles	205	28½			5843				5843	—	—				58.43	3542	✓	58.43						
18	Harold Tank	205	34			6970				6970	—	550				64.20	3543	✓	69.70						
19	Robert Timmerman	320	28			5600				5600		90				55.10	3544	✓	56.00						
20	Arnold Kurth	180	28¾			50.85				50.85	—	680				44.05	3545	✓	50.85						
21	Marvin Manders	170	28¾			5083				50.83	—	220				48.63	3546	✓	50.83						
22	George Hansford	242 247	4½ 24	4½		121 5938	62			61.11	—	—				61.11	3547	✓			61.11				
23	Gabriel Diederich	247	16			3952				3952	—	—				39.52	3548	✓			39.52				
24	Harvey Lemerond	247	28¾ 7¾			7101	587			7688	—	460				72.28	3549	✓			76.88				
25	Felix Gollaer	247	24			5928				5928	—	610				53.18	3550	✓			59.28				
26	Emil Elm	253 247	1		1136	353 155			10110	10548	—	320				103.28	3551	✓			105.48				
27	Arthur Kramer	247	16			3952				3952	—	—				39.52	3552	✓			39.52				
28	Alvin Borkovec	247	24¾ 3¾			6113	93			6206	—	—				62.06	3553	✓			62.06				
29	Julius Borley	247	48			11856	Vacation 12/31			11856	—	1190				106.66	3554				118.56				
30	Frank Berg	247	24¾ 4½			5910	31			6021	—	170				58.51	3555	✓			60.21				
31	Gaylord Bricco	242 247	24		1136	121 155			10110	106.69	—	1010				96.59	3556	✓			106.69				
32	Vernon Plouff	242 247	24½		1131	121 155			10110	109.16	—	550				103.66	3557	✓			109.16				
33	George Koltz	253	4½		568	127			5055	51.82		230				49.52	3558	✓			51.82				
34	Edward Langenberg	242 247	19¼ 24½	4½ 1	568	303 20.58	61 123		5056	7709	—	230				74.77	3559	✓			77.09				
35	John Trybula	247	48			11856	Vacation 12/31			11856	—	130				111.26	3560	✓			118.56				
36	Harold Van den Avond	246 247	11¼ 5		504	2768 1235			4423	8768	—	870				78.98	3561	✓			87.68				
37	Clifford Rodgers	247	19¼ 1¼			1681 25.55	216			105.13	—	174				72.23	3562	✓			105.73				
38	Richard Becks	246 247	14½ 4½		252	2291 23.47	62			7540	—	330				72.10	3563	✓			95.40				
39	Elmer Anderson	247	16			3952				3952	—	—				39.52	3564	✓			39.52				
40	Robert Linexens	207	1½			1967				1967		120				18.47	3565	✓	19.67						
	TOTALS THIS SHEET															846.52									
	BALANCE FORWARD FROM PRECEDING SHEET															1046.20									
	TOTALS																								

CHAPTER FOUR:

NOW IS THE TIME

"Don was a genius in coming up with ways to convince the ICC that Schneider could provide unique service," says longtime Schneider General Counsel Tom Vandenberg. For example, he had the trailer manufacturers eliminate a lip at the top of the doorframe, providing a larger opening that allowed beverage-can shippers to put an extra row of cans in the trailers even though the trailer dimensions hadn't changed.

It took Don Schneider just a year and a half to plow through Wharton's notoriously rigorous curriculum. He was eager to get going with his career. There was a place for him at Schneider Transport, but he wasn't certain he wanted to work for his father. "He planned to interview with companies on the East Coast," says Pat Schneider, "but one night he got a call from his dad. He said he needed help, so we returned to Green Bay."

Soon after returning to the company, Don was contacted by a St. Norbert professor who invited him to teach part time. He began teaching an 8 a.m. finance class before going to his full-time job at Schneider Transport. Within a year, he was teaching two classes. At St. Norbert, he honed the fair but demanding management style he would use at Schneider. When he got the impression that some students were spending more time socializing on Friday nights than he considered appropriate, he began scheduling tough exams on Saturday mornings. The students who responded positively to this rigor caught his eye.

Don liked teaching, but the workload, along with his Schneider job, was crushing, so in 1966, he left academia and focused entirely on Schneider Transport. His arrival brought the company's office staff to five, but he was far more than just another worker. Almost from the beginning, it was clear he would take the company to another level. Military service and the Wharton School had made him a leader to be reckoned with.

DON GEARS UP FOR GROWTH

Bright and energetic, Don set about aggressively acquiring new authorities for Schneider. "As Don found more and more work, I would find a way to move all the products," says brother Paul Schneider, who joined the company in 1962 as operations manager, a job he would hold for four years. Don saw Schneider Transport as a business with immense unrecognized potential. No opportunity to develop new business or save money was too insignificant to escape his scrutiny.

With Don on board, Schneider Transport began to

The snub-nosed, cab-over trucks, opposite, that Schneider used in the 1970s and '80s were not favored by many drivers. Mounted on a short wheelbase, they could be a rough ride — noisy, too, with the engine churning beneath the floorboard. Their blunt face was anything but aerodynamic, reducing fuel efficiency. The tractor air shield sports the company's stylized "S" logo, which it began using in 1962.

At the University of Pennsylvania's acclaimed Wharton business school, Don Schneider invested himself wholly, grinding through the tough curriculum in just a year and a half. He wasn't sure what future lay before him, but he couldn't wait to get after it. As things turned out, he was preparing himself to utterly transform his father's business.

grow in ways it never had before. ICC permission was required to expand operations at the time, and that required proving that existing services provided by other carriers were inadequate. "Don was a genius in coming up with ways to convince the ICC that Schneider could provide unique service," says Tom Vandenberg. For example, he had the trailer manufacturers eliminate a lip at the top of the doorframe, providing a larger opening that allowed beverage-can shippers to put an extra row of cans in the trailers even though the trailer dimensions hadn't changed.

Don's efforts to improve the company sometimes rubbed his father the wrong way, though. Al had built Schneider Transport, and it wasn't always easy to watch his son change the company even though the professional acumen Don brought with him was a tremendous asset. As Don's role in the business expanded, the "old man," as many of his longtime employees fondly referred to him, often felt marginalized — not least because Al, just 51 the year his son joined the business, wasn't that old.

"Don was very different from Al," notes Wayne Lubner, who joined the company in 1971 and became one of its most prominent leaders. "Al would get mad about something, and he'd go and scream at someone. Everyone knew that in a little while he'd mend the fence. Don was a systematic thinker and a great marketer but not warm and fuzzy. You could feel his intensity in every transaction."

Dave Schneider, meanwhile, felt like he was treading water at the company. He wasn't making progress and felt little inspiration to invest in the business. "One day in 1963," he remembers, "Don said to me, 'You're not happy working here, are you?' I told him I wasn't, and he said, 'There are some permits

---

UNIVERSITY of PENNSYLVANIA

PHILADELPHIA 4

GRADUATE DIVISION OF BUSINESS
AND GOVERNMENTAL ADMINISTRATION

Wharton School of Finance & Commerce

February 25, 1960

Dear Mr. Schneider:

Good scholars are always a great credit to a school and are the principal creators and sustainers of its reputation. The quality of your work in the Fall semester deserves recognition and thanks. I am pleased to have your name appear on the Honor List.

Sincerely,

D. F. Blankertz
Director

available right here in town that you should look into.'"

Dave took his brother's advice and launched his own business with a truck and permits from Jones Transit to haul cheese out of state and carry return loads for the paper industry. Within a few years, he had leveraged that single truck into two and ultimately a fleet of 18. "It felt good to prove to my dad that I could do it on my own," Dave remembers. "I know he was proud of me."

ACQUISITION AND EXPANSION

Thanks to Don's efforts, business was soon so brisk that the company was chronically short of trucks to handle the work. Paul Schneider frantically juggled equipment and drivers to stay on top of demands. More than once, when an International Truck salesman loaned the company a new truck to test, Paul put it to work hauling loads. "One time, we used the test truck so much that we had to buy it," he says.

In the autumn of 1963, Schneider purchased Packer City Transport, which had 16 drivers and a small terminal on Buchanan Street in Green Bay. Packer City handled a substantial volume of local cartage, but it was also an interstate freight operation, moving paper and food products to 12 Midwest states and carrying glass and building materials as return loads. Though Packer City was not a huge company, its acquisition increased Schneider's interstate operations, setting the stage for future growth.

One of the first drivers Schneider hired to augment the existing Packer City workforce was a young man from Green Bay named Gary Lautenslager. He was 28 and had been working in a Menasha, Wisconsin, paper mill, but "that wasn't for me," he would recall years later. "I wanted to be a trucker."

He only made one trip for the company, though When he got his first paycheck and had to cash it at Tilkens Bar, he worried about Schneider's stability. He quit and joined another Green Bay trucking company. Over the next four years, he worked for several more. Each went out of business.

By the time he returned to Schneider on June 20, 1968, he was a more seasoned driver, older and a bit cynical. He was pleased to find that Schneider had evolved. "It was a much more successful business," he says. "That time, I knew I had found a home." He could not have imagined just how long he would remain with the company.

Among the many things that had changed at Schneider by the time Lautenslager returned to the company was its relationship with the union. On Wednesday, January 15, 1964, a cold day in Chicago, the trucking industry had agreed to the first National

By 1962, Schneider Transport's old logo, seen on the trailer below, looked dated. In May of that year, the company introduced the "S" logo seen on page 52, with arrowheads on each end — a more contemporary look signifying Schneider's growing capacity to haul anything anywhere.

like a public utility, and it created a monopoly."

Despite the union's increasingly cumbersome restrictions, Schneider Transport continued to grow. In 1966, Schneider took over Weyerhauser's fleet in Marshfield, Wisconsin, establishing its first group of drivers west of Green Bay. That operation mostly involved long-haul freight with semi trucks and flatbed trailers, but Schneider added drivers to cover the needs of paper shippers and meat companies in western Wisconsin.

As his economic muscle grew, Don Schneider made more major acquisitions. In 1968, he bought Garrison Transport to obtain authorities and expand rapidly. Garrison, with about 60 independent contractors, was based in Fowler, Indiana. Schneider closed the Fowler facility, replacing it with a dispatch office in a house trailer on a vacant industrial lot in Streator, Illinois, 90 miles to the northwest.

Dick Schluttenhofer, who had been a rate analyst for the Western Trunk Line Committee, an agency that regulated about 12 railroads in Chicago, came to Schneider with Garrison. He accepted an offer to join Schneider in Green Bay, even though he was first assigned to the old Packer City Transport facility. It was a cavernous metal shed — cold as a barn in winter, sauna-like in summer and reeking with diesel fumes — in which dispatchers and customer service people sat at folding tables clustered together on a concrete floor, across which ran a spaghetti of telephone cables.

Schluttenhofer reported to Neil DuJardin, who had joined Schneider with the Packer City acquisition. DuJardin began as a rater, determining costs for different loads of freight. He rapidly rose through the ranks to the position of vice president of inside sales and pricing. He put Schluttenhofer to work as a payroll supervisor and rater, but it didn't take him long to conclude that in the Garrison refugee he'd inherited a boatload of experience.

Garrison's primary authority was to carry glass

Master Freight Agreement (NMFA) with the Teamsters. Ensuring standardized pay and benefits for more than 450,000 American drivers, it affected some 16,000 carriers. At that point, "Labor relations became like pro wrestling," says Vandenberg. "Contracts would last three years, then there would be a national strike. New contracts with rate increases would be negotiated, approved by the ICC and forced on carriers and shippers. The model was

containers from Illinois and Indiana to Wisconsin breweries. "Schneider had permits going south and east," explains Schluttenhofer. "When they bought Garrison, it gave them the back haul."

Acquiring the back haul, a load that made both legs of the trip profitable, was extremely important. Schneider was beginning to master the process of efficient supply-chain management. Not only did that distinguish successful transportation companies from the rest of the pack, it also signified the start of a robust national network for Schneider.

Also in 1968, Schneider reopened its public storage business and purchased Kampo Transit, a 50-truck regional milk and fuel oil hauler with bases in Neenah, Wisconsin, and Chicago Heights, Illinois. Kampo marked Schneider's entrance into the bulk (tanker) business. Kampo's name was changed to Schneider Tank Lines, and it formed the foundation of what would become Schneider National Bulk Carriers, a division of Schneider National that now transports liquid bulk specialty chemicals all over North America.

Paul Schneider was Schneider Transport's director of safety, driver personnel and industrial relations when the company bought Kampo. Though safety had always been a Schneider priority, Paul's appointment to this position formalized it as a company concern. The job was especially important because the U.S. Department of Transportation (DOT), formed in 1966, was performing increasingly detailed, safety-oriented inspections. A higher standard of recordkeeping became necessary, since the DOT could stop carriers from getting authority if their records didn't pass muster.

With about 40 drivers and some $6 million in sales, Kampo "had terrible, old equipment and a rundown building in Neenah with an old tractor-and-trailer shop and an inadequate yard," says Paul. He was surprised when it soon became his mess to fix.

JIM AND JOHN CLIMB ABOARD

By the late 1960s, Al Schneider's youngest sons, Jim and John, had followed in their older brothers' footsteps, trying their hand with the company. They had paid their dues cleaning warehouses and running errands. Both knew how to drive trucks, and once they had their drivers' licenses, they also became licensed as truck drivers, earning money during vacations.

After graduating from high school, John enrolled at the University of Wisconsin. Every summer, he worked for his father's company, primarily hauling paper products. When he completed his undergraduate work, he spent six months in the Schneider tire shop before enrolling

Military experience in the 1950s shaped Don Schneider's worldview as well as the management model he refined at the Wharton School and on the job at Schneider. In the 1960s and '70s, experience as a military leader was almost a requirement for Schneider management recruits; a generation of young officers, many of whom had been Don's business students at St. Norbert College, became Schneider leaders. Opposite, Sonny Wagner, a longtime Schneider driver, stands in front of a Kampo Transit truck. Schneider purchased Kampo in 1968, expanding into the bulk, or tanker, business. The 50-truck milk and fuel oil hauler had bases in Neenah, Wisconsin, and Chicago. Schneider changed Kampo's name to Schneider Tank Lines, and it was the foundation upon which the company's National Bulk Carriers division would be built.

in graduate school. He earned his master's degree, then gave the company one more try. For a summer, he worked for Paul, driving tanker loads of wet peas from Neenah to Milwaukee. But his heart wasn't in trucking. After he moved to California to complete a Ph.D. in clinical psychology at Stanford University, he never returned to live and work in Green Bay.

For Jim, the story was different. Though the work his father gave him as a teenager at first seemed crushingly boring, he found ways to define each task as uniquely his own. He set personal standards, greater than what was expected, and eventually "came to love working there." After a tour with the Army, stationed in Virginia as a transportation officer, he returned home and drove a truck for his father while attending classes at the University of Wisconsin-Green Bay on the GI Bill.

He completed his undergraduate work and gave graduate school a shot, but he says, "I didn't want further education. I wanted to work." He returned to the company, working his first jobs in dispatching and customer service. He remained with the company, gradually working his way up the ladder, but it would be many years before he finally found his place in the organization.

A NEW APPROACH TO STAFFING

Don wanted to do more to grow Schneider than merely acquiring other businesses. He was determined to grow a culture for the future. To do that, he needed a new breed of managers, and he liked the military model. To find them, he engaged the recruiting firm Lendman Associates, which held job fairs across the country, targeting military officers of the sort that Don Schneider sought. Most of Lendman's clients were large national and multinational businesses. Later on, Schneider worked with another recruiter, San Francisco–based Career Seminars. In contracting the services of those companies,

By the 1970s, Schneider Transport was growing rapidly, and the old McDonald Street building, where the company had been located for nearly 30 years, was no longer adequate. In September 1971, Schneider moved its headquarters to a more spacious building at 2661 South Broadway in Green Bay. McDonald Street and several other Schneider outposts remained open.

Road Angels

In 1976, Ralph Stoffel was driving Schneider trucks on a route from Wisconsin to the West Coast and back. One Friday night that winter, as he passed through Omaha, Nebraska, he encountered one of those fierce, wind-driven snowstorms that churn across the Great Plains.

Stoffel, who'd been driving for Schneider for five years, had been lucky with winter weather up to that point. "I'd always rationalized that, if I'm headed west and the storm is headed east, I would get through it faster if I just kept going," he wrote years later in his memoir, *Staying for the Long Run.*

The storm he encountered that evening did not abate, though. By 8 p.m., when Stoffel reached Grand Island, Nebraska, about 150 miles west of Omaha, the weather had become so bad that traffic ground to a halt. Fortunately, he had fueled up in Des Moines, reasoning there was a good chance he'd be spending the night stranded on the highway. Setting the truck on a fast idle to keep the cab warm, he crawled into the bunk and monitored the radio for news about the weather.

"About midnight, someone was knocking on my door," he recalled later. "I couldn't believe it when I saw a young woman with a child, standing up to her hips in a snow bank. I opened the door, and she told me that her car had shut off and she had two small children and wondered if I could help her."

Stoffel helped the lady and her kids into his cab and then trekked to her car to retrieve food and diapers. No sooner had he rescued the young family from the storm than an elderly couple knocked on his door, also seeking shelter.

It was early Sunday morning when rescue workers with snowmobiles and sleds in tow finally arrived and transported Stoffel's guests to safety. Stoffel remained on the highway four more hours before crews finally cleared enough snow for him and other motorists to get under way. Even then, he had to drive another 150 miles before he finally escaped the storm.

"I thought about all the people who didn't get to a truck cab for safety," Stoffel said. "I later heard on the radio that seven people died that weekend in their cars from hypothermia or carbon monoxide poisoning."

Ralph Stoffel is hardly unique among Schneider drivers who've been road angels. In 1985, Grant Warnick Jr. rescued a pregnant woman from a burning van. In 1991, William "Butch" Click, a Schneider driver from Charlotte, North Carolina, rescued eight people who were trapped in a burning camper that had been struck by another truck near Nashville, Tennessee.

Over the years, many Schneider drivers have found themselves in a position to help others and they've consistently stepped up to the challenge — not because it's company policy but because it's the right thing to do. "I didn't do it for any other reason than … to help people," Click said.

Schneider trucker Ralph Stoffel hosted two families in his cab over two long winter nights near Grand Island, Nebraska, in 1976 while a powerful blizzard snarled across the Great Plains. Stoffel is one of the many Schneider "Good Sams" who've gone out of their way to help other motorists in trouble over the years.

Schneider was unique, not only among businesses its size in Green Bay but in the trucking industry as a whole.

A generation of young men and women bred with the same fundamental values as Don and refined by military service joined Transport over the next decade and left upon it an imprint apparent to this day. The first of those young managers was Wayne F. Baudhuin. A farm boy who'd been a gridiron standout at St. Norbert College, he was one of several hard-working, levelheaded students who'd impressed Don during his brief teaching career. Baudhuin joined Schneider Transport on September 1, 1968, as operations supervisor, reporting to Paul Schneider.

Mike Weiss, who would become operations manager, was another St. Norbert graduate and former military officer whom Don hired. Weiss recalls that his interview with Don lasted nearly two hours. For the first 45 minutes, Don asked him questions. Then he spent an hour talking about the company and its potential, as though testing whether Weiss had the right stuff to play a role in converting Don's vision to reality. The young man had just gotten his first taste of Don Schneider's intense, demanding style.

By the end of 1968, it was clear why Don wanted such leaders on his team. Schneider Transport had limited authority to operate in all 48 of the contiguous United States, and although the company had grown significantly through important acquisitions, Don Schneider was just getting started, and he needed a team that was up to the tough challenges that lay ahead.

TEAMSTER TROUBLE IN BULK

For a year after acquiring Kampo, the only significant change Don Schneider made to that company was to change its name. The business was losing money, however, and in 1970, Don sent Paul to check on it. Don needed someone he could trust in Neenah. Paul

reluctantly took over Schneider Tank Lines, never imagining he'd be with it for the next 18 years.

Chief among Kampo's problems was the Teamsters union and its local leadership. Kampo, a regional carrier, had become unionized in 1965, and the union leaders opposed the Schneider long-haul model. They wanted local union drivers to pick up freight and bring it to Schneider's over-the-road drivers, who would take over for the line-haul to a location near the freight's final destination. Once the load was there, union drivers would step in again and do the local delivery. The union demanded this process for both vans and tankers. It was

Bill Frisque, Schneider's IBM hardware engineer, worked with computer operator Marlene Olejniczak in the early 1980s. Computers revolutionized Schneider, and for a time, hardly a week went by when some new computer enhancement didn't make operations more efficient and productive.

The production area where Mark Owen, above, worked was the forerunner to today's Customer Service department, though it was a decidedly smaller place than the immense bullpen pictured on page 117. Schneider drivers donned suits and ties to attend annual banquets such as the one, opposite, circa 1960. A way to extend the company's gratitude to its drivers and acknowledge members of the Million Mile Club, exemplars of safe driving, the banquets continue to this day.

an enormous inconvenience whose only purpose was to keep local union drivers employed, and it was a sticking point in contractual negotiations again and again.

Schneider's strategy for the bulk business was to gradually win concessions from the union while setting up new operations wherever they could. One of the first outposts was in Blooming Prairie, Minnesota, where Paul acquired authority to haul a Viking Chemical Company compound used to manufacture plastics.

There was, however, a reckoning with the union about the bulk operation that Schneider would not be able to avoid. The bulk drivers in Chicago Heights were members of Teamsters Local 705, Louis "Louie" Peick's operation. Peick had joined the union in 1931 and earned his stripes on the meanest of streets. In 1947, he'd been kidnapped and tortured by a gang of men who forced him to open a union safe and give them $25,000. Three years later, two thugs had accosted him in front of his home, beating him with a baseball bat and shooting him.

The attacks just made him tougher. He ran Local 705 as his private kingdom. Negotiating with him was inevitable, and when it finally happened, says Paul Schneider, it was "a nightmare."

SCHNEIDER'S FIRST SALES TEAM

Don's next acquisition, in 1970, was Lavery Transport, which had regular-route, general commodity authority between Green Bay and Chicago, allowing the company to tack on several more authorities. Even with simmering union tensions and higher costs, Schneider rode the growth of the trucking industry to new heights. The company boasted 400 drivers and $13 million in revenue and was moving quickly to exploit progress in the construction of the Interstate Highway System and the increasingly poor service of the railroads.

Don realized the time had come to create a field sales force. The man he selected in 1971 to head it was Don Martin, who came from Hormel Foods, the Minnesota meat-processing company. Martin quickly assembled an effective team to handle sales in dedicated regions. Calm and soft-spoken, he proved to be "a great relationship builder," says Paul Schneider.

With Paul dedicated to Bulk, it was necessary to find a new head of personnel and safety. Don recruited another of his former St. Norbert students, Don Jauquet, who had earned his MBA from the University of Wisconsin in 1967. In the Army, Jauquet had served as a military police officer. At Fort Leavenworth, Kansas, he was a custodial and personnel officer. Jauquet joined Schneider Transport on June 1, 1970, as assistant personnel and safety director with responsibility for driver recruiting. In the coming years, he would play a key role in union relations that involved contract negotiations and a sweeping program to educate unionized associates about the changing business environment and its impact on the company and their livelihoods.

Among the attendees at the company's annual banquet circa 1960 were "Budd" Elm, first row, sixth from right; Merlin Lardinois, first row, third from right; Roger Klein, second row, second from right; Al Schneider, third row, far right; and Clarence Schneider, fourth row, far right.

If Al Schneider had a safe haven, it was the company's shop. He loved to rub shoulders with the mechanics who kept his fleet rolling. Trucks of this era had shortened bumpers that did not wrap around the front tires — a strategic design intended to prevent damage to the tires if a deer and the bumper of a big rig went head-to-head on the open highway. Opposite, Wayne Lubner, left, confers with colleagues Harley Piper and Bob Treptow. A Wisconsin boy homegrown on a farm, Lubner had an instinct for transportation. He rose through the company's ranks to senior management positions and played important roles during the deregulation of the industry and the launch of the union-free company, Schneider National.

THE "SCHNEIDER SMILE"

In 1971, Schneider Transport was granted sweeping authority to haul just about anything related to paper manufacturing. Unprecedented for the time, it covered a vast, 11-state area stretching from Minnesota to Pennsylvania, Tennessee and West Virginia. The crescent route from Green Bay to the Eastern states, south of the Great Lakes, became known as the "Schneider Smile."

The company's growth rate was practically out of control now, outstripping existing systems and resources. In one year, revenues leaped from $13 million to $23 million. To handle the growth, Schneider made two major changes. It acquired its first computer, an NCR unit that was used to track all sorts of data — from sales to drivers' miles and hours — and expedite processes ranging from payroll to load rating. It was considered to be cutting-edge, and Myles "Mike" Burcham, manager of data processing, and program analyst Ken Viet used it to develop the company's first electronic data management system, the Computer Assisted Real Time General Operations System (CARGOS). The next big change was a move in September to a new, larger building at 2661 South Broadway in Green Bay. McDonald Street and other Schneider facilities remained open, and it was clear that Schneider needed the space.

Sometime after the company moved into the Broadway terminal, Al and Don convened a meeting of drivers and told them Schneider was going to install "communications" — telephones — in their cabs. Like most of the drivers, Lautenslager was skeptical — feeling the company had been slow to upgrade equipment or fix problems in the past. He remembered the day in 1969 when he was returning from Indiana in one of the blunt-nosed, cab-over trucks — never popular with drivers — that Schneider was experimenting with at the time. He'd just crossed the Illinois border when he broke a front leaf spring, causing the cab to lean acutely to the right.

Lautenslager had no alternative but to limp back to Green Bay, more than 180 miles, in that awkward condition.

Lautenslager liked driving for Schneider, but, even in the face of driver complaints, equipment and technology hadn't improved much in the decade since Borley and Elm blazed the trail to Cheboygan. "We drove a lot of the trucks that were junk," Lautenslager says, bluntly. "They *all* leaked when it rained."

Every driver also knew what it was like to call dispatch for information about their loads. They had to find a rest area and then stand in line with a bunch of other truckers — often outside in punishing weather — to use a pay phone. To Lautenslager, Don Schneider's pledge of "communications in your trucks" sounded like mumbo jumbo.

As things turned out, Don's promise was a bit premature, but he was true to his word. He knew that communications technology wouldn't be just a convenience for his drivers. It would give his company a powerful edge over the competition.

Growth through acquisition continued. In 1972, TransNational Truck (TNT) of Amarillo, Texas, became part of the Schneider enterprise. TNT's primary freight was meat from Texas and Kansas bound for the East Coast. Departing from the earlier practice of integrating all acquisitions into Schneider Transport, the company kept the nonunion TNT as a separate business unit. Already, Don Schneider and his leadership team could foresee a day when it would be necessary to sever relations with the Teamsters. Key to achieving that was building a separate, nonunion division of the enterprise.

The more Schneider grew, the clearer it became that all roads led to or through Chicago, an important stop on the "Schneider Smile" where trucking, shipping and railroads converged. Sooner or later, Schneider would have to come to grips with the Teamsters' Louis Peick. In 1973, invoking Teamsters "law," Peick demanded that

Schneider Transport stop delivering freight to Chicago and use his drivers to pick up and deliver Chicago freight from the old Kampo depot in Chicago Heights.

It was a predictable demand. If Schneider complied, it meant a lot of extra work for drivers in Peick's local. Peick had the clout to make things tough for Schneider and, given the strategic importance of Chicago, his edict could not be ignored.

Don and Paul Schneider, with Don Jauquet, went to Chicago to meet Peick on his turf. Accompanying them was Milwaukee attorney Tom Duffey, head of the Wisconsin Motor Carrier Labor Advisory Council, which heard grievances in Wisconsin. Duffey had spent several years as an employer trustee of the Central States Health and Welfare and Pension Funds. That he enjoyed good relationships with senior members of the International Brotherhood of Teamsters made him exceedingly useful to Schneider.

At Peick's office, the team was buzzed into a waiting room. Presently they were allowed through a second checkpoint. At last, they were summoned to Peick's office, a vast room in which he sat, like an emperor, behind a desk approximately the size of Comiskey Park. Peick was a compact man with sandy hair shading toward frost. He squinted at Don Schneider through his glasses and then, almost before his guests had been seated, slammed his fist on home plate and screamed, "There's no way in hell I'm going to allow your drivers to deliver in our area."

From that high point, the meeting went downhill. In the end, the Schneiders struck a conditional deal: they would comply only as long as Peick's demand was applied to all other trucking companies. For the next two months, Paul Schneider stayed in Chicago, a sleuth chronicling the comings and goings of competing carriers. There were so many that not even Peick could bar them all from making deliveries. Schneider quietly resumed direct pickup and delivery.

LABOR AND FUEL TREMORS

Like many Schneider associates, Wayne Lubner grew up and learned to drive on a Wisconsin farm. By the time he enrolled at St. Norbert, where he wrote an acclaimed paper about maintenance systems, he was, in his words, a "transportation guy." After graduating in 1971, he served two years in the Army. On July 2, 1973, less than a month after he was discharged, Schneider hired him as a night-shift supervisor. Three months later, he moved to a service team, working on trucks, a job he held for the next two years.

He found a friend and mentor in fellow veteran Wayne Baudhuin, who helped Lubner acclimate to the company's culture. Late in the 1970s, after a stint as a Midwest division manager, Lubner was named Schneider's safety manager for four rapidly growing states: Indiana, Michigan, Illinois and Ohio. He stayed in that job for a decade and eventually retired after serving on the senior leadership team for several years.

Schneider was growing at a brisk 10 to 15 percent annually by then, and Lubner was "charged with hiring drivers to meet demand; developing, coaching

By the middle of the 20th century, Al Schneider, the gear jammer who'd gambled his family's future on trucking, had parlayed the one truck he acquired in 1935 into a transportation empire and reinvented himself as a savvy businessman in the bargain.

and mentoring new leaders coming into the company [and] developing the values, skills and promotable characteristics Schneider was [seeking]." He found himself playing an important role in relations with the Teamsters that would become increasingly contentious as regulatory changes beyond the control of either the union or Schneider altered the way the industry operated.

Late in October 1973, the members of the Organization of Arab Petroleum Exporting Countries

proclaimed an oil embargo in retaliation for the United States' decision to resupply the Israeli military during the brief Yom Kippur War. With fuel shortages driving up costs and the federal government imposing a nationwide, 55-mile-per-hour speed limit, the United States' dependence on Middle East petroleum was made starkly clear even before the embargo triggered a recession that would drag into 1975 and beyond, affecting every aspect of the economy.

Schneider was inspired to seek a reliable fuel supply. In 1977, the company purchased Green Bay–based Christensen Oil from Herb Hoeft, a friend of Don's. Now working for Schneider, Hoeft was put in charge of fuel and tire procurement. While competing companies paid retail prices, Schneider could now buy bulk oil. That same year, Schneider opened the company's first bulk fuel site at the Wise Garage in Dayton, Ohio, laying the foundation for what would become the Schneider National Fuel System, with more than 100 fuel locations.

Though the oil embargo ended in the spring of 1975, the recession it had triggered lingered on, and the company began looking for efficiencies to mitigate its impact. Chief among them, thanks to the company's NCR computer, was online billing. Practically science fiction by the technological standards of the time, the concept was to generate freight bills by computer and send them to customers while shipments were en route. "We are a company striving not just for growth but for increased efficiency and service to our customers," wrote Jim Schneider, in a National Transportation Week edition of *Keep On Truckin'*, an early Schneider newsletter.

The company also decided, again, to get out of the warehouse business and focus on freight transportation. It didn't have much difficulty finding a buyer for its Green Bay warehouses. The new owner was Leicht Transfer and Storage, the company Julius Borley had driven for before he joined Schneider. Underscoring Schneider's commitment to hauling freight, the company acquired National Refrigerated Transport, Inc., of Tulsa, Oklahoma, and added it to its growing list of subsidiaries in 1974.

THE STORM ON THE HORIZON

In the spring of 1976, when the Teamsters' National Master Freight Agreement was up for renewal, the union mounted a three-day national strike over monetary issues. Before drivers would return to work, Schneider Transport was obliged to sign an agreement to abide by the NMFA.

That June, a Schneider delegation met with union personnel in Chicago, where Schneider agreed to a new pay method. The agreement alienated some drivers who felt they had a better deal under the previous compensation formula.

When they learned of the new agreement, 12 Green Bay drivers, who came to be known as the "dirty dozen," led their own five-day wildcat strike from June 26 to July 1. Schneider fired the drivers, including Gary Lautenslager, for their action, but Al gave them a second chance. "Al Schneider met with us and offered reinstatement if we signed an agreement to never go on a wildcat strike again," says Lautenslager, who was grateful to get his job back. "I signed right away."

Union problems persisted, though. In August, when Schneider employed 1,000 drivers for the first time, company personnel were back in Chicago for seven more grueling days of dawn-to-dusk, tooth-and-nail negotiations after thousands of Teamsters drivers filed grievances over the compensation requirements of the new NMFA. Don Jauquet characterized the experience as "hell week" and said it was "the single most challenging event … we faced during our 30-year transition from [union to union-free]."

While this was going on, Don Schneider, unofficial head of the company for five years, was formally named president and chief executive officer of Schneider Transport. It was a year of major milestones. The company's revenues reached $82 million. The online billing system went live and was a big success, reducing processing time from 18 days to just two, and several new operating permits allowed Schneider's van operations to expand the company's paper business into most of the Midwest, the East and parts of the South. Though the Teamsters continued to make noise, business was healthy and promising.

It was at about this time that Schneider Tank Lines decided to concentrate on chemical hauling and get out of the bulk milk business. When the company acquired authority to move a special resin that had to be maintained at 300 degrees Fahrenheit throughout the trip, Paul Schneider created National Bulk Transport and had special tankers built with a system that circulated heated liquid through coils in the belly of the tank.

By 1977, Schneider had consolidated its nonunion subsidiaries under a single holding company, American National Corporation (AMNACO). It embraced SMS (Schneider Moving & Storage), TNT (TransNational Truck, Inc.), NRT (National Refrigerated Transport, Inc.), WNI (which had been intended to be Western National, Inc., although that name was unavailable) and NBT (National Bulk Transport, Inc.). AMNACO owned 100 percent of the outstanding stock in each of the companies in the organization.

AMNACO's creation had a greater meaning, however. It was a signal that Don Schneider was battening down the hatches in preparation for a storm that he saw brewing on the horizon: deregulation and the related need to move away from Schneider's longstanding relationship with the Teamsters.

Don Schneider took over the family trucking company from his father in 1976, and no one was more responsible than he for transforming it into the giant, logistics-driven international transportation machine that it is today.

CHAPTER FIVE

EVERYTHING
LOOKED
UNEARTHLY

> "What I found unusual was how Don instilled his core values in the company," Ernie Micek recalls. "A trucking company tends to have a lot of turnover, but Don drove the values into the business. At almost every meeting of the board, he'd make a little speech and he would direct it especially at his executive team. He'd say, 'We have to do better than our competition. If we can't deliver better value, we don't deserve the business.'"

Schneider Transport quickly outgrew the expanded offices it had occupied for barely seven years on South Broadway. Associates had spilled over to various buildings, including the old McDonald Street complex. In response, the company relocated its administrative offices in 1978 to 3061 and 3051 South Ridge Road in Green Bay, side-by-side buildings (which Schneider later connected to create 23,800 square feet of space) owned and previously occupied by Employers Health Insurance. Schneider's operations and maintenance remained at South Broadway.

The year brought Schneider more than a change of address. It marked the start of a newly competitive approach to business. Don Schneider made that point clear in a 1978 speech to associates, identifying eight small to mid-sized carriers to whom the ICC had recently granted authority to haul Wisconsin paper products to 48 states. Don considered the Wisconsin paper companies, most of them based in Green Bay, to be Schneider customers. "The commission gave these carriers the authority to encourage competition," Don said. His point: Schneider had to be vigilant and service-oriented if it was to keep its customers.

A NEW EMPHASIS ON TECHNOLOGY AND ENGINEERING

Schneider had just come off another record year. Achieving sales of more than $94 million in 1977, it had moved up from its 1976 position of number 53 (with $89 million in sales) to number 46 on *Commercial Carrier Journal*'s list of the top 100 Class 1 Carriers — but Don knew better than to take anything for granted in his volatile industry.

The success might be only momentary if he didn't take steps to ensure that Schneider remained competitive. Don realized the transportation companies of the future would need more than just large fleets. They had to be technologically astute. Acquiring state-of-the-art technology meant attracting a top-notch engineering team.

Larry Sur had joined Schneider the previous summer in the capacity of what today would be called chief information officer, having spent 12 years in engineering and systems positions with Whirlpool Corporation. An energetic man who was always thinking of new opportunities, he tackled Schneider's technology deficiencies immediately.

Attired in the blue jeans and denim shirt that became something of a uniform for him late in his storied career, Don Schneider personified the visionary cowboy — but he was first and foremost a tough-minded businessman.

On the bank of the Fox River, Schneider's South Broadway complex, above, blanketed over 21 acres in the early 1980s. Broadway was the last place where all of the company's Green Bay operations were consolidated in a single location.

Sur spotted trouble right away. For all the hoopla surrounding the installation of CARGOS only a few years earlier, Schneider's information technology (IT) system was so outdated that a team of full-time associates was required just to convert drivers' logs into computer punch cards so drivers could get paid. To make matters worse, Schneider had just signed a five-year contract with NCR, manufacturer of the computer around which CARGOS was built.

Sur swiftly took action to extricate Schneider from the NCR deal, replacing the computer with a new IBM 360/60 computer, then he led a team of IT professionals that designed the $1 million Schneider Online Utilization Resource (SOURCE) system. SOURCE made it possible for Schneider to track the movement of every tractor, trailer and driver and cross-reference them with customers, load types and loaded and empty miles driven. When SOURCE went online in January 1979, it

was just what the company needed.

If CARGOS could have become obsolete so quickly, Don reasoned, then other systems could be out of date, as well. So, in 1978, he formed an engineering team to evaluate all of the company's equipment and technology. The goals: determine how to improve what Schneider had and enable better purchasing decisions.

The first task was to change the specifications for tractors in order to make them more efficient on the road. Schneider adopted common industry specifications for engines, brakes, fuel-efficient tires, power steering and aerodynamic roof shields, and within six months, costs had been significantly cut.

KEEPING THE TRUCKS ROLLING

Schneider's 30,000-square-foot shop on Broadway was a busy place, with 25 tractor bays, six trailer bays and six bays for repairs that needed fast turnaround. The shop was constantly full, and eight mechanics were assigned to two shifts daily just to rebuild engines for the Schneider fleet.

Fearful that the Teamsters might try to organize mechanics in remote locations, Schneider handled repairs to trucks on the road through contracts with independent garages. It was up to Larry Chaplin, recently hired after completing seven years of military service as a captain, to crisscross the Midwest, ensuring that service was up to Schneider's standards. Chaplin initially was a member of a Schneider team that managed the maintenance relationships, but in time he would become director of the Schneider National Maintenance System, one of the nation's largest networks of heavy truck repair facilities.

If you were trying to find Al Schneider, the South Broadway shop was the place to look. With Don running the company, the breakneck pace of the enterprise's unfolding future was leaving Al, like many first-generation entrepreneurs, behind. To his sons Jim and John, he confided that he felt Don was trying to take the company away from him — and there was more than a little truth to those assertions.

"Don loved his dad, but he found it hard working with him," says Don's wife, Pat Schneider. "I know how much he respected what Al had built and how hard Al worked to build it, but they were very different. It was an uneasy relationship."

More and more, Al gravitated to the shop, where he felt at home. Equipment repair was a mostly cut-and-dried process, with few annoying ambiguities.

THE FOUR-LEGGED PLAN

In the spring of 1978, the ICC issued a ruling designed to discourage the inefficient operation of trucks, especially running bobtail (without a trailer) or hauling empty trailers. The decision was propelled by the energy crisis, and as though to prove the members of the commission

foresighted, a second fuel shock occurred. Schneider Transport responded by establishing the Schneider Fuel School and mounting a national campaign to teach its 2,000 drivers to conserve fuel by driving 55 miles per hour.

The ICC's actions notwithstanding, most signs that year suggested to Don Schneider and his team that the industry was about to be deregulated. The implications were immense. Deregulation meant removal of the old, authority-based constraints around which the trucking industry had been built and with which Schneider had always lived. Many of the nation's 20,000 registered motor carriers were small, union-free operations. In an open market, they would be able to dramatically undercut Schneider and union carriers on rates. The company's management realized that Schneider's success was dependent on the simultaneous development and implementation of a new long-term strategic thrust.

Don Schneider's team came up with a four-legged plan. The first three legs called for continued expansion of the customer base; improved driver relations combined with education and career development for associates; and a rapid expansion of union-free operations, either through independent contractors or with company drivers. Some of this work was already under way. For example, the SOURCE information system had made the company more efficient and capable of growing the customer base; *Pumpkin Press*, Schneider Transport's first employee newsletter, which had debuted on March 15, 1976, was an early effort to communicate directly and consistently with associates.

The first three legs of the strategy called for hard work on aggressive schedules, but they paled in comparison to the magnitude of the fourth: withdrawing from the Teamsters agreement — and the sooner the better. Deregulation would change everything; of that Don was certain, and he also feared that the union's

Though he was the man atop the Schneider empire, Don Schneider was never too busy to take time for new associates. An introduction to the company and its unique culture began on their first day on the job, and Don, like his father, felt that no one was better qualified to handle that task than he.

restrictive work rules and high-cost structure would spell the company's doom in a deregulated environment. Don believed Schneider had to convince the union to allow it to exit the National Master Freight Agreement and to decrease its participation in the oppressively expensive Teamsters' Central States Health and Welfare and Pension plans. The NMFA and the Central States plans were former Teamsters' President Jimmy Hoffa's signature accomplishments. No company had ever successfully exited either, and the Teamsters knew that if they allowed Schneider to leave, others would follow.

Still, Don persevered. He knew that failure to exact those concessions from the Teamsters would, over time, render the company uncompetitive. Until deregulation, Schneider had been a successful company, and many wondered why, at a time when the company was healthy and growing, he would put that at risk by going toe-to-

toe with the union as business conditions were changing. His answer: "If the union was going to make it impossible to compete, I wanted to know that sooner rather than later. I wasn't interested in a prolonged going-out-of-business sale."

STAFFING UP FOR DEREGULATION

Ensuring that the company would survive deregulation was the challenge Don Schneider issued to Ed Thompson. A native of Oregon who had earned a degree in engineering from Oregon State, Thompson was Procter & Gamble's local division manager. He had a reputation as an innovative and successful manufacturing operations manager. One day in 1979, Don invited him to lunch and made a proposition.

"Don told me, 'Ed, we're going to be facing a threat,'" says Thompson. "'I want you to help me turn it into an opportunity.'" Trouble was, Thompson was committed to a new job at P&G. He was relocating to Cincinnati and had gone so far as to buy a new house there. He was more than intrigued with Don's job offer, though. He loved a good challenge, and as Don described to him what lay ahead for Schneider, he knew it was an opportunity he couldn't turn down. By the end of 1979, he had sold the Cincinnati house and become the new president of Schneider Transport. Don remained president of the holding company.

Paul McCarthy also began his career with Schneider Transport that year. With a B.S. in mechanical engineering and an M.B.A., both from Cornell, military service as an artillery officer and a decade of general management experience, McCarthy brought Schneider expertise in operations, customer service, business planning, engineering, purchasing and maintenance. He initially was named manager of corporate business planning, but within a year, he became vice president of operations. He soon moved up to the ladder to executive

A representative of the International Brotherhood of Teamsters solicits support from others, including at least one Schneider driver, in this photograph from an issue of *Time* magazine in late 1973. From the 1940s on, the Teamsters were a force to be reckoned with — that is, until 1980 when Don Schneider and his management team realized things had to change if the company had any chance of surviving deregulation.

Don's Library

Don Schneider's office at Schneider headquarters was a remarkable place for its lack of chairs. A man of boundless energy, Don worked standing up. He felt that by staying on his feet, he got more done. Meetings were shorter and more pointed, as well. No one who was obliged to discuss something with him wasted much time when there was no opportunity to lean back and relax.

Relaxing was something Don didn't do very well. Even when he was home at night, he was never far removed from his work. The television, his sons recall, was often tuned to national weather so that he could track meteorological phenomena that might impact the business. Beside his armchair was a stack of business periodicals, industry journals, reports, newspapers. Many mornings, when he returned to the office, he would take with him pages torn from those publications that he was anxious to share with members of his staff.

Perhaps nothing was more revealing about Don's intellectual interests, however, than the short shelf of business books published during the 1980s and 1990s to which he referred again and again as he strove to shape Schneider for the "long haul." They included such classic volumes as John P. Kotter's *A Force for Change*, Ronald A. Heifetz' *Leadership Without Easy Answers*, and Benjamin B. Tregoe and John W. Zimmerman's *Top Management Strategy*. Each was heavily annotated with Don's margin notes.

Chief among those books, dog-eared and extensively underlined, was *Built to Last*, Jim Collins and Jerry I. Porras' account of their six-year-long study of 18 major companies that shared, among their distinguishing characteristics, both success and longevity. Don called it the "Schneider Bible." It was effectively a blueprint for durable corporations, packed with examples of how those businesses stayed vibrant after so many years.

Durability was, arguably, Don Schneider's most

Built to Last, which Don Schneider called the "Schneider Bible," stands out among the shelf of business books Don regularly consulted during the 1980s and '90s as he strove to design a business that would endure long after he was gone.

fervent hope for the company. Hardly a day passed when he didn't refer to *Built to Last*, in which he found inspiration over and over as he plotted the future of a great American company that he knew full well would long outlast him.

vice president of operations and served in a key role on Thompson's leadership team.

Don moved to bolster his legal team, as well. If lawyers had played an important role in the company during the regulated years, they would be just as important as the company moved to break free from the Teamsters. In 1979, the general counsel at Schneider was Charles "Charlie" Singer, who had begun working for Al Schneider years earlier out of his office in Fort Lauderdale, Florida. Singer's associate was John Patterson, who had joined the company in the mid-1970s.

"Since so much of the legal work involved hearings that were held in front of administrative law judges at various U.S. district courthouses, having the legal department in Florida to accommodate Singer wasn't illogical," says Tom Vandenberg. "Flights were more readily available there than in Green Bay."

Patterson, however, saw deregulation on the horizon and pushed to relocate the department to Green Bay, where its services could evolve as a more traditional corporate legal department. Considerably younger than Singer and less invested in the regulatory practice, he made a compelling argument, and the team moved to Wisconsin in 1980. Vandenberg, just admitted to the Wisconsin State Bar, had since joined the department.

Singer and Patterson were only in Green Bay a short time when the union attempted to organize the company's mechanics. With the help of outside counsel, Patterson managed to beat back the assault. It wasn't much of a skirmish, but Patterson could see that the future of the company depended upon a different labor-management relationship. "Labor was where the action was, and Patterson jumped in with both feet," says Vandenberg.

In 1983, when Charlie Singer resigned from Schneider and returned to Florida to establish a private legal practice in estate planning, Patterson was named

general counsel. He remained in that position until 1987.

If it wasn't clear to Ed Thompson what he was getting into before 1979, it certainly became clear when Transport participated in multi-employer negotiations for the Iron and Steel and Special Commodity contract, a supplement to the National Master Freight Agreement, early in 1980. A major sticking point was how drivers would be compensated. Schneider and other carriers advocated a system like the one Schneider had negotiated with the Teamsters in 1976, in which compensation was based on a percentage of the value of the load being hauled.

Don Jauquet, Transport's representative in those negotiations, recalls, "… the Teamsters called a [10-day strike] on certain carriers, including Transport, almost all of whom had a representative in the negotiations. [It] negatively impacted our customers and caused Transport to lose … credibility." It cost the company a lot of money, too. As if that weren't enough, some Schneider drivers mounted their own 10-day wildcat strike from April 28 to May 7, 1979.

Gary Lautenslager, who'd learned his lesson back in 1976, abided by his promise to Al never to engage in another wildcat action. He kept his job while others were not so fortunate. Schneider fired 80 drivers, including some other members of the "dirty dozen." There were grievance hearings, and the cost in legal preparation and representation was huge; but in the end, the matter served a valuable purpose for Schneider: making it clear that the company was serious about doing whatever was required to compete in the changing full-truckload marketplace.

The struggles with the Teamsters throughout the 1970s had made Schneider Transport tough. Repeated work stoppages only made young Schneider managers, tempered in military service, more determined to win. "The drivers would just walk away and leave their

Ed Thompson was Procter & Gamble's local division manager in Green Bay when Don Schneider hired him in 1979 as president of Schneider Transport. An innovative operations manager, Thompson joined Schneider on the eve of deregulation and helped lead the company through that tortuous transition as well as the escape from the stranglehold of the Teamsters union.

Engine repair and replacement has always been a high priority in Schneider shops. As long ago as the 1970s, two teams of mechanics were assigned to that task in the company's South Broadway shop, and they worked two full shifts every day to keep up with the demand.

vehicles, regardless of what they were hauling," says Larry Chaplin. "A bunch of us would go out and find the trucks. We'd hot-wire them and proceed to make the deliveries, with Wayne Baudhuin dispatching back in Green Bay. People would be yelling at us and throwing things. It was like war."

MOVING AHEAD WITH PURPOSE

On Sunday, December 2, 1979, Anne Curley's lead story in the business news section of *The Milwaukee Journal* was headlined "Truckers in Turmoil" and it opened with an unequivocal declaration that "The trucking business in Wisconsin is in the midst of an unprecedented shakeup." The 48-year-old Neuendorf Transportation Co. had just agreed to sell out to a Detroit-based conglomerate, Curley reported, a move that came on the heels of the sale of LaCrosse-based Gateway Transportation Co., then Wisconsin's largest trucking operation, to a Canadian company.

Deregulation, Don Schneider told the journalist, was inevitable. Contract carriers "have been deregulated, for all intents and purposes," he said. "Ninety-eight percent of the applications that the ICC receives for operating authority are being approved. The competition has intensified dramatically."

Seven months later, on July 1, 1980, when President Jimmy Carter signed into law the Motor Carrier Act of 1980, deregulation was little more than a formality. Still, Carter noted, and rightly, "This is historic legislation. It will remove 45 years of excessive … government restrictions and red tape. It will have a powerful anti-inflationary effect, reducing consumer costs by as much as $8 billion each year. And by ending wasteful practices, it will conserve annually hundreds of millions of gallons of precious fuel. All the citizens of our nation will benefit."

Carter also opined that deregulation would "create greater flexibility and new opportunities for innovation"

in the trucking industry. As anticipated, a school of upstart companies — J. B. Hunt, Swift, Heartland, MS Carriers and Werner — emerged as though their tractors had been quietly idling, waiting for the garage doors to be thrown open at the stroke of Carter's pen. They were ravenous as piranha, and standing between them and a payday were Schneider Transport and the other established carriers.

Don knew that his industry was not the only one undergoing extraordinary change. In a February 24, 1992, *Fortune* magazine profile of the Schneider president, Myron Magnet wrote, "The big retailers and manufacturers [Schneider] served were resolutely slashing inventory costs by installing just-in-time delivery systems. Without bulging warehouses, they increasingly needed shipments *now*." Magnet further observed, "When big interstate truckers emerged blinking into their brave new deregulated world after 1980, everything looked unearthly to them."

"A lot of people in the industry were paralyzed with

While not popular with Schneider drivers, cab-over trucks offered a distinct maintenance advantage in that the cab housing could be tilted forward easily, giving mechanics especially convenient access to the engine compartment.

A forklift operator loads pallets of Bounty paper towels on a Schneider trailer. Key to Schneider's growth and durability was that Al Schneider and, later, Don, forged successful, long-term relationships with major American paper products manufacturers, including Procter & Gamble, Kimberly-Clark and Georgia-Pacific, during the company's early years.

fear," says Vandenberg, "but Don moved ahead with purpose." While many competitors scrambled to regroup, Schneider and Ed Thompson were already hard at work.

In order to compete with the upstarts, the company had to land new business at the same time it shaved costs. Meanwhile, in the intensely competitive deregulated marketplace, the prices that trucking companies could charge their customers plummeted. If there was any question that deregulation was having an impact on Schneider, one needed to look no further than the candid, two-page memorandum concerning the "State of Our Business" that Thompson sent to all Schneider Transport managers and administrative employees on June 11, 1982. Stating his commitment to do "what is necessary to keep … Transport a profitable, healthy and growing company," he wrote: "The combined effect of heavy competition and excess capacity flowing from deregulation has translated into very serious rate cutting … This has resulted in an operating loss of $3,500,000 over the past seven months. This is not acceptable. We are committed to being profitable in 1982. We will not allow the strong financial position we have built to be eroded through losses."

Thompson's memo outlined a series of steps the company would take to trim expenses, including an immediate cut in management pay, a 10 percent reduction in all operating budgets, a hiring freeze, elimination of unauthorized overtime compensation and the allowance of capital expenditures only with the written approval of a company vice president.

By the time he issued that memo, Thompson was already working with accountant Don Cope to build a "key factor management system," a schematic similar to one he'd used at Procter & Gamble that showed all of the company's cost factors — by customer, by type and by region — to streamline budgeting decisions. Thompson had also beefed up Schneider's sales force, growing it

In 1981, Jim Schneider launched a transcontinental operation called American Pacific Express to move freight across the United States from busy West Coast ports. He later sold the business to Schneider National, which changed the name to APX. Working out of the company's old McDonald Street facility, Jim continued to run the operation through the 1980s. When he left Schneider in 1990, he was the last of Don's siblings to depart the company.

from two salespeople to 60 in two years. To make such growth possible, he had hired James Liebig in 1980 as Schneider's first vice president of human resources. Liebig was a pioneer in innovative hiring and education practices and the development of self-managing work teams.

With his new sales team aggressively beating the bushes, Thompson drove Schneider's business growth at a steady rate for several years during the mid-1980s. "We also went out and actively sought big-name customers like Kellogg's and Kimberly-Clark," says Thompson. Offering Schneider's tradition of reliable service at dramatically reduced rates, "Don told them, 'We want all your business.'"

In the pursuit of that business, the company's growing technological proficiency was a significant advantage. As a Schneider marketing document from the early 1980s observed, "Our industry is unique. It runs on 'real time.' We have no inventory of stored services to use when demand peaks. Therefore, we must … plan well for the peaks and valleys of demand. We do not have any lead time. Our data needs to be massed quickly, and decisions need to be based on available data in order to optimize equipment and manpower. The computer has helped us greatly in this area."

A NEW APPROACH WITH THE TEAMSTERS …

Those actions kept the company's head above water, but there was still the issue of the Teamsters union.

"The company's approach had been to ignore the unions and deal with them over grievances," Thompson recalls. He believed that Schneider National would have more success with a proactive rather than reactive approach — communicating openly with unionized employees, explaining the economics of the deregulated environment and engaging them to help the company thrive — which was, after all, in their mutual best interests. Thompson taught Schneider leaders like

Baudhuin, Lubner and Jauquet new tactics for negotiating without provoking hostility. "I told them to tell the union the truth, over and over and over," he says.

It was in Schneider's interest, as well as that of the associates, for the company and union to get along. Between 1976 and 1979, there had been five strikes against the company, each one elevating customers' concerns about Schneider's reliability. At a time when on-time delivery was becoming more important than ever, Schneider couldn't afford to be seen as unreliable, and any loss of business would affect union members' jobs.

When Teamsters officials threatened to put the company out of business if Transport didn't meet their demands, the even-handed Schneider response was, "Yes, you have the ability to do that, but such an action would benefit no one — company, drivers or Teamsters. Rather than waste time, let's discuss the problem and collaborate to save Teamsters jobs."

Internally, the company launched a series of weekly drivers' meetings. Groups of 20 to 25 drivers spent two days at headquarters for updates aimed at helping them better understand the business and thus better contribute to the company's success. People from all areas of the company, especially scheduling and dispatching, attended those programs, as did Al Schneider, who always came to talk with the drivers.

Training was not just for drivers. Thompson realized it was essential to train everyone at the company in order to build the world-class operation Schneider desired to become. He recalls, "We were growing, bringing on people, trying to change old behaviors and reinforce good business habits."

… LEADS TO A NEW LABOR AGREEMENT

In 1981, Jim Schneider, who had spent more than a decade in the company without ever feeling like he'd truly found his place, launched his own enterprise. Called

American Pacific Express, Inc., it was a transcontinental operation designed to rapidly move truckloads of products from increasingly busy West Coast ports to the companies in the Midwest and on the East Coast that were importing those products.

At last, Jim had found his niche. He threw himself into American Pacific Express with an entrepreneur's passion, and it was soon a success — so much so that barely a year passed before Don Schneider was negotiating with his younger brother to bring the operation under the Schneider tent.

While that was going on, Schneider's holding company, AMNACO, was renamed Schneider National Incorporated. Schneider Transport, the old unionized company that Al Schneider had created, still existed, but it was now separate from Schneider National Carriers, a union-free business. The days when Schneider was constantly at odds with the union were nearly over. As fewer union drivers joined the Transport workforce, Schneider National Carriers continued to grow in the deregulated world.

Though the company still owned a large fleet of tractors and trailers, an increasing number of drivers were owner-operators. Schneider formed a new entity to help them purchase their own equipment and opened an innovative driver training center to ensure that all new drivers had the skills to get behind the wheel of a Schneider rig. Even drivers with years of experience were tested before they could operate company equipment. Schneider's safety standards, always improving, were far more stringent than those at many competing carriers.

The ICC granted Schneider 49-state authority to carry all commodities except explosives, and in 1981 the company moved a record 290,000 truckloads. Revenue hit the $200 million mark. Still, the cost of running a huge national transportation business was astronomical, and with rates now sharply trimmed, it became harder

and harder to make money. It was in that context that the company left the National Master Freight Agreement in 1982, negotiating an individual labor agreement with the Teamsters.

"It was essential to exit the NMFA," says Vandenberg, "but doing so was generally thought to be impossible. The Teamsters were deathly afraid that if anyone was able to exit, there would be increasing pressure for others to leave, until the whole structure collapsed."

Compounding the problem was a piece of legislation, passed by Congress the same year as deregulation, called the Multiemployer Pension Plan Amendments Act (MEPPA). It affected all participants in the Central States Health and Welfare and Pension Funds. MEPPA created a new liability for trucking

Without the hard work of Don Jauquet, Tom Vandenberg, Ed Thompson, Wayne Baudhuin, Wayne Lubner and Don Schneider, left to right, Schneider might not have survived deregulation of the trucking industry in 1980. They developed and deployed the plan to transition from the unionized Schneider Transport to Schneider National Carriers, a union-free business built to survive in the 21st century.

The Million Mile Club

Retired Schneider driver Duane Livermore, one of a number of former drivers who also served as tour guides at Schneider's headquarters, tells a cautionary tale for any young driver who aspires to membership in the company's storied Million Mile Club. To become a member, you must not only drive a million miles — a feat that would take more than 75 years if one drove the national average of 13,000 miles per year for motorists. You must also drive a million miles without having any accidents.

Livermore's initial run at club membership failed just short of the mark. He had accumulated more than 900,000 miles when he backed into a mailbox. It wasn't even his fault — the person who was guiding him into position at the time failed to tell him about the mailbox — but in Schneider's safety-conscious world, an accident is an accident, and Livermore had to start back at zero miles. Even though Schneider long-haul drivers cover many more miles every year than the average motorist, it still takes them years to reach a million miles. Livermore eventually made it.

Perhaps the most high-profile embodiment of Schneider's rigorous adherence to a culture of safety, the Million Mile Club was introduced in 1985. It testifies to the quality of Schneider drivers and the safety training they get as part of the job — and it's a badge of honor that by 2010, when Schneider celebrated its 75th anniversary, more than 4,000 drivers had made it into the club. Their collective

In 2011, Mark DeSotel, above, who first climbed behind the wheel of a Schneider National truck in 1976, became the third driver in the company's history to log more than four million consecutive, accident-free miles. He joined Bob Wyatt, who accomplished the feat in 2009, and George "Sonny" Wagner, who set that standard back in 1997. In 2012, Michael Pott became Schneider's fourth four-million-mile driver. Connie and Ronald Hamilton, opposite, are also members of Schneider's Million Mile Club. Connie is one of nearly 600 women who drive for Schneider.

achievement amounts to over two billion miles of safe driving.

George "Sonny" Wagner accomplished the staggering feat four times. The first Schneider driver to log more than four million accident-free miles, he set the bar in 1997. Three other Schneider drivers have matched the achievement since then: Bob Wyatt in 2009, Mark DeSotel in 2011 and Michael Pott in 2012.

Livermore is also part of this small cadre of remarkable drivers. His dedication to Schneider — and that of road warriors like Merlin Lardinois, Bernie Watzka, Vern Johnson, Roger Klein and Julius Borley — has transcended the road. Long past their driving days (a collective 222 years), they stayed active and provided valuable service as cheerful and deeply knowledgeable tour guides at the Green Bay headquarters for a combined 105 years. All told, they logged 327 years of service to Schneider National.

Al Schneider began his career as an independent contractor, so it's not surprising that Schneider National still has a soft spot for independent truckers. Mike Turner, posing with his truck, above, is one of more than 2,000 drivers who own their own rigs, many of which were financed with help from Schneider Finance.

companies that exited such multi-employer pension plans. The company that tested the law faced a liability in the millions of dollars.

"MEPPA forced companies that were unable to adapt to the post-deregulation competition to remain in business as long as possible in the hope that the new law would be declared unconstitutional or something else would change," explains Vandenberg. "Congress allowed new entry into the industry at the same time that it created a very real barrier for many companies to exit. The result was overcapacity, and the downward pressure on prices was extreme."

Even if Schneider could find a way to exit the NMFA while satisfying the requirements of MEPPA, there were

big questions about what a replacement collective bargaining agreement would look like. No template existed.

The solution that Schneider created was the Special Services Division (SSD), a separate bargaining unit within Schneider Transport. Though they were members of the union, new drivers hired to work in the SSD were covered by Schneider's benefits plans, not the Central States plans. John Patterson, who collaborated with Ed Thompson, Don Jauquet and others on the creation of the SSD, spent hundreds of hours with Jauquet drafting and revising the new agreement.

Jauquet and Baudhuin then visited all of Schneider's Teamsters locals for face-to-face meetings about the changes in the industry and how those changes were affecting Schneider's relationship with Teamsters drivers. "We gave them the economics of the truckload industry," recalls Jauquet. "Customers viewed Schneider Transport as high-cost, inflexible and subject to disruption. This was in no one's best interest. Some people understood. Others were stubborn."

In the end, a majority of Schneider's Teamsters drivers approved the new labor agreement. That and other factors enabled Schneider to trim costs by $1 million in 1981. The agreement also ensured that union drivers could keep their jobs and benefits as the company transitioned to a union-free workplace. To Don Schneider's credit, he was determined not to abandon them. They had helped make the company what it had become, and he felt he owed them. Still, by 1985, Schneider significantly slowed hiring in the SSD and accelerated hiring in Schneider National Carriers. Within two years, the number of drivers in Schneider National Carriers equaled or exceeded those in Transport.

Some of the Teamsters remain at Schneider today — Don's approach to survival in the deregulated market having saved their jobs. In the early 1980s, when

The Schneider Online Utilization Resource (SOURCE) system was a powerful tool for planning and dispatch workers such as Carolyn Peeters in Green Bay. Developed in the 1970s by Chief Information Officer Larry Sur and a team of information technology professionals for the company's new IBM 360/60 computer, SOURCE enabled dispatchers and customer service personnel to track every vehicle and driver and cross-reference them with customers, load types and loaded and empty miles driven.

By 1982, Schneider had so many WATS lines that it could profitably sell telephone service to other businesses. Don Detampel, below, turned this capacity into a subsidiary called Schneider Communications that was a success from the moment it was introduced.

everything was on the line, Schneider was the only trucking company to approach deregulation in that progressive way. Of the top 100 for-hire carriers in 1980, the year of deregulation, only 15 exist today — and of all the unionized truckload carriers that existed in 1980, Schneider is the only one still in business.

PBX AND NITRO TO THE RESCUE

The 23,800-square-foot facility on South Ridge Road had seemed generously sized when Schneider moved into it in 1978, but the company quickly outgrew it. In 1982,

Schneider migrated again, completing a phased move into a 102,000-square-foot building nearby.

Coincident with the move, Larry Sur and his team were working on another major project. This one involved the telecommunications system, and it made life better for Schneider customers and drivers alike. The only way Schneider had to "quickly" communicate with both groups in the early 1980s was via the landline telephone network, and it wasn't quick at all. Customers would call in on Schneider's inbound wide area telephone service (WATS) network and provide instructions for their loads; drivers would call on a separate network and ask for their next dispatch. Every call went through a bank of operators at an antiquated switchboard, and it was at that point that one-third of customers' calls and half of drivers' calls got dropped. For a company that promised reliable freight service, it was a huge problem.

Sur's team addressed it by installing an AT&T Dimension 2000 — a private branch exchange, or PBX, telephone system uniquely configured for Schneider's needs. Installing the PBX was "scary," says Don Detampel, who had built a strong working relationship with Sur on the computer conversion and was given a lead role in upgrading Schneider's telecom system. Since the phone system was the company's lifeblood, there could be no transitional downtime. With the help of Bell Laboratories, Detampel and John Straub, who managed voice communications, created system architecture similar to what the phone company used in its central office. The project took months and involved considerable training of personnel; but once the Dimension was in place, the lost calls dropped to less than 1 percent for customers and 5 percent for drivers.

The new system also allowed Schneider to buy very high WATS line capacity, further improving service for drivers. That, in turn, spawned NITRO

Don Detampel, left, general manager, and Gary Madden, sales manager, look over telephone switching equipment that will be used in a long distance telephone service to be marketed by a new company, Applied Communication Systems Inc., a subsidiary of Schneider National. The equipment is located in the Schneider Transport Co. plant on South Broadway.

Press-Gazette photo

New telephone service offered

A new long distance telephone service for businesses that could reduce costs by 25 to 40 percent on out-of-state calls will be marketed by a subsidiary of Schneider National Inc.

The new firm is Applied Communication Systems Inc. Don Detampel has been named general manager.

Schneider is a Green Bay-based holding company formerly known as American National Corp. (AM-NACO). It was formed in 1976. The name was changed to Schneider National Inc. in August 1981. Among the companies it owns is Schneider Transport Co.

vice president of Sch-

Applied Communication now have the authority to provide telephone services such as the one being introduced to Brown County businesses, Sur said.

Applied Communication is one of the largest users of Bell's Wide Area Telephone Service (WATS) in the Midwest.

Because of the large volume of long distance calls it handles, the company receives substantially lower telephone rates. Those reduced rates will be passed on to customers of Applied Communication.

Beginning in October, that service will be offered to other businesses located in Brown County.

NITRO uses a Dimension Custom

The company has more than 200 circuits and now handles more than 300,000 calls a month.

Sur said there is no limit on the potential expansion of the system.

The telephone switch has been equipped with uninterruptible power and duplicate computer processors to insure reliability of the system.

Detampel explained that connection to the Allied network can be action complished from any push button telephone.

In addition to linking with the long distance service, the company will provide its customers with a management reporting system for the analysis and comparison of phone costs and a credit card replacement service.

— New Improved Telephone Resource Operation — which allowed drivers to make calls directly to central Schneider operators on inbound WATS lines. Previously, they had been forced to make expensive credit-card calls. It wasn't the in-the-cab communications Don Schneider had promised drivers earlier in the decade, but it was a big step forward. It saved a lot of money, too.

NEW REVENUES THROUGH ACQUISITIONS – AND COMMUNICATIONS

In 1982, in helping one of its major customers better manage its shipping operations, Schneider played a big role in what became one of the milestones in the evolution of modern supply-chain technology. The customer was the giant Minnesota-based corporation, 3M, and the problem Schneider helped it to solve was a consequence of the corporation's great size. With plants and distribution centers widely disbursed around the world, 3M had no choice but to let every facility make its own shipping decisions. There was no synergy whatsoever.

With Schneider's help, 3M created the world's first load control center. Schneider engineers adapted the company's mainframe software to help 3M centralize inventory and shipments between its 120 plants. Efficiently coordinating carriers and routes, the new software enabled 3M to expedite shipping and reduce costs. It would be a few years before large numbers of companies followed 3M's lead, but when they did — especially after the Gulf War, which brought the importance of logistics into clear view — the 3M model soon became the industry standard. Schneider suddenly found itself inundated with requests for help from other companies that wanted to learn how to better manage inventories and shipping schedules. Pioneering better technological solutions, Schneider was quickly redefining itself as a leader in supply-chain management.

Schneider found another creative way to make money in the early 1980s. Thanks to the Dimension 2000, Schneider had become Wisconsin's second largest user of wide-area telecommunications service. By 1982, it had 247 WATS lines and was paying about $15 million to Wisconsin Bell for long-distance service, making the company eligible for volume discount rates. When the Federal Communications Commission lifted restrictions on the resale of WATS service that year, Schneider was well positioned to buy long-distance telephone time in bulk and resell it to other Wisconsin companies.

Don Detampel realized this was a potential gold mine that no other company in the state was better equipped to exploit. With Sur's help, Detampel developed a business plan. Don Schneider approved it, and that summer, the new business became a reality with Detampel at its helm. Initially, its name was Applied Communications Systems, but it would later change its name to Schneider Communications. A success from the outset, it began with three employees serving 15 customers. By the end of 1982, there were 135 customers, and the new business was just scratching the surface.

In October 1982, while Detampel was getting his new business up and running, Jim Schneider struck a deal to relinquish his ownership of American Pacific Express to Schneider National in return for stock. He would remain in charge of the business, which operated out of the company's old McDonald Street facility. Also in 1982, the company took its first steps in the dedicated business with bulk equipment.

Early the next year, Schneider was about to complete its headquarters move, keeping South Broadway as an operating center and ultimately purchasing the buildings it had been leasing from Employers Health Insurance. The company began that year in an enviable position. Having survived the first years of deregulation, it had reinflated

When Al Schneider succumbed to a heart attack on the afternoon of Wednesday, March 2, 1983, Ed Thompson circulated this memo to all Schneider associates. "We have lost a friend, a supporter and a strong contributor," he wrote. "Let's keep him proud of us."

its figurative tires and was confidently rolling down the highway. It had finished 1982 with record-breaking sales of some $300 million and was operating more than 2,700 tractors and 4,600 trailers.

All of the trucks were being retrofitted with a device called Tripmaster, which monitored and evaluated fuel utilization. It tracked speed, RPM and idle, helping the company identify inefficient vehicles and drivers so that either could be remedied. The company did not yet have the technology to remotely access the data, but that was right around the corner. In the meantime, drivers

were continually trained on fuel conservation and safety. Having to manually extract and turn in their Tripmaster data ensured that they got the message to slow down and conserve. It would be eight more years before technology, in the form of a device called SensorTRACS, would automate the remote collection of essentially the same data.

"LET'S KEEP HIM PROUD"

Al Schneider was nearly 76 as 1983 began. His colorful career in the trucking business spanned almost half a century. If he was a man given to historical reflection, though, he had never displayed much evidence of it. From the minute he got behind the wheel of his first truck, he seemed steadfastly focused on the future. Determination and resilience had enabled him to rise from humble origins to lay the footings of a successful American company, and there would have been no better time to look back than upon his 48th anniversary.

Unfortunately, he didn't have the chance. Al began the day on Wednesday, March 2, with his usual routine. In the office early, he soon was prowling the shop. But in the middle of the afternoon, he came out of his office and announced that he didn't feel well and was calling it a day. He never made it home. Witnesses who saw what happened said that as he neared an intersection near his home, he slumped over the steering wheel. His car slowly drifted off the street, down a grassy embankment and came to rest against a highway fence. He was dead of a heart attack by the time a local couple stopped their car and tried to help him.

The next morning, the beginning of a dark day at the company, Al's passing was front-page news in the *Green Bay Press-Gazette*. Ed Thompson spoke for everyone in a memo circulated companywide. "We have lost a friend, a supporter and a strong contributor," he wrote. "He cared and respected us as individuals. We were his driver

SCHNEIDER TRANSPORT

SCHNEIDER®   414-497-2201   P.O. Box 2298   Green Bay, Wisconsin 54306

March 3, 1983

Dear Fellow Employee:

It is indeed a sad day for Schneider Transport employees. Al Schneider, our founder, chairman of the board and good friend died of an apparent heart attack Wednesday afternoon. I don't have to tell you how much he cared about Schneider Transport and each of its employees. He regularly expressed his personal feelings as he talked with you individually and met with you at meetings and driver banquets. He was proud of your accomplishments and thankful for your loyalty and friendship. This was especially true over the last three years - years made very difficult by deregulation and the poor economy.

I wish each of you could have experienced the pride he felt as he observed your exemplary performance during the recent independent truckers strike. He was especially pleased with the way the whole organization was working together and commented several times on how good it was to see and feel our people, his people, pulling together.

We have lost a friend, a supporter and a strong contributor. He cared and respected us as individuals. We were his driver group, his mechanics, his administrative team and his managers. Most of all, we were his friends and the people he counted on to keep his number one love, Schneider Transport, healthy and growing. He has now passed this challenge on. Let's keep him proud of us.

Ed Thompson
Ed Thompson

Under blue skies, a pumpkin truck rolls across the Leo Frigo Memorial Bridge, the highest in the Green Bay area, across which Interstate 43 first spanned the Fox River in 1981.

group, his mechanics, his administrative team and his managers. Most of all, we were his friends and the people he counted on to keep his number-one love, Schneider National, healthy and growing. He has now passed this challenge on. Let's keep him proud of us."

DOOR TO THE FUTURE

There was nothing to do, of course, but to keep on, and in 1984, the company did so in a big way. Schneider had absorbed many companies on the path to becoming one of the world's largest transportation businesses, but it didn't have an open-equipment division. That August, Schneider bought one: International Transport of Rochester, Minnesota.

Heavy-load haulers typically handle super-sized equipment such as construction prefabrications, jumbo boilers and oversized power transformers. International Transport was the nation's largest such company. It had done $85 million worth of business in 1983, moving equipment for the agriculture, construction, glass and steel industries, and rolling stock for John Deere, Case and two of the Big Three automobile manufacturers. To ensure its success, Schneider also purchased International Transport's Trailer Services, Inc. subsidiary, which rebuilt and maintained trailers.

In another technological advance, Schneider began

A Schneider National truck pulls past a row of trailers on its way out of a Schneider operating center in the 1980s. Schneider opened its first remote operating center in 1986 in the small Ohio farm community of Seville. The $6 million facility, opposite, bottom left, housed four dispatchers, each assigned to a cadre of Ohio-based drivers, and featured a host of amenities for drivers and a state-of-the-art shop. It was the template for a network of service centers that soon opened across the United States.

Don Schneider and his wife, Pat, to his left, found a moment of tranquility in the woods near De Pere, Wisconsin, in the early 1980s with their children, left to right, Mary, Tom, Kathleen, Paul and Therese. Though Don was a restless perfectionist dissatisfied with the status quo and always looking to improve operations at every level, the photo opposite shows the face of a contented man whose work informed his life and who was wholly capable of appreciating the magnitude of what he achieved as a giant of the modern transportation industry.

using Micro Dispatch Aids, software that analyzed factors such as cost and location to recommend load assignments, maximizing utilization of drivers. State-of-the-art technology was revolutionizing the business, enabling pinpoint decisions based on an accurate analysis of facts rather than on gut instinct.

Planning was also now under way for Schneider's first company-owned remote operating center. Don and Al had long resisted building a company shop network, fearful that the Teamsters, which had tried to organize the mechanics in 1980, would try again. By 1984, however, with Schneider's move to a fully union-free company accelerating, Don was ready to build operating centers across the country. This was partly intended to reduce costs and improve customer service, but mostly it was an attempt to create a supportive, open-door culture for drivers in light of the changing workforce.

Don initially committed to building 10 operating centers. They'd seek to improve the road experience

for drivers, providing them with a relaxing environment featuring good meals, a lunchroom and TV lounge, fitness and laundry facilities, hot showers, vending machines stocked with sandwiches and salads, and other amenities. As Schneider associates interacted eye-to-eye with drivers at the centers, the company could better understand what they thought about their jobs and whether they had any needs and concerns that the company could address.

"We wanted a more human experience, an experience in driving for Schneider that was different from driving for anyone else," says Wayne Lubner, "and we wanted a culture where people didn't feel like they needed someone else to talk for them."

For its first center, a prototype for all the others, Schneider chose Seville, Ohio, a small community in rolling farmland 25 miles west of Akron and 50 miles southwest of Cleveland. The property Don Schneider and Lubner had discovered was strategically located along the "Schneider Smile," just off Interstates 71 and 76. Construction began in early 1985, the same time the company was in the process of adding 17 more truck stops to the Schneider National Fuel Network.

The Seville center opened in September 1986. With a Goodyear blimp circling overhead, Don Schneider addressed a large group of associates, customers and dignitaries. "This industry … requires long hours … and a very demanding commitment to quality service," he said. "And that's one of the values you find in our people. We try to make that job as easy as possible."

Designed from scratch over a period of 18 months by Schneider associates, led by Steve Parent and collaborating with a Green Bay design firm, the new facility cost a bit more than $6 million. It had four dispatchers, each assigned to 100 Ohio-based drivers, and it had the capacity to handle many more. Overhead fueling stations, grease pits similar to those in quick-lube automotive garages and an automatic rising scaffold for making trailer roof repairs made it state of the art. Workers on break could relax in air-conditioned comfort, and drivers had a comfortable home away from home.

Seville was an unqualified success, and in just a few years, a network of operating centers spanned America in such far-flung locations as Charlotte, North Carolina; West Memphis, Arkansas; Indianapolis, Indiana; and Fontana, California. Seville also formed the model for teaching future leaders about the operational side of the business and served as the springboard from which many would launch career paths that led to the corporate office. Mark Rourke, for example, began his Schneider career at Seville as a team leader, went on to launch a dedicated B. F. Goodrich account, one of the company's early wins in the new Dedicated business, and later rose through the ranks to become president of Truckload Services.

Within five years, the operating centers allowed Schneider to convert 80 percent outsourced maintenance to 80 percent company maintenance. In the process, according to Larry Chaplin, Schneider "dramatically lowered our maintenance expense and improved equipment reliability and uptime." The real value of the operating centers, however, lay in improved relationships between Schneider and its drivers, in how drivers felt respected and valued by the company — and that would be essential as Schneider moved ahead with its post-deregulation business plan.

The impact of Seville at a crucial transition in the trucking industry was so significant that Daniel P. Bearth, who covered the opening for *Transport Topics*, described the facility as Schneider's "Door to the Future" — and he couldn't have been more right.

CHAPTER SIX:

WORLD WITHIN REACH

A logistics management pioneer with a full complement of transportation modes at its disposal, the little trucking company Al Schneider founded in Green Bay, Wisconsin, in 1935 has built bridges across the world.

As the first decade of the 21st century unfolded, it became clear that the long-haul market was shrinking and supply chains were moving ever closer to customers. In the changing market, the logistics business appeared more important than ever.

As though some great gear had shifted, Schneider picked up speed as it hurtled across the borderline of a radically changed industry. Several years into deregulation, as competitor after competitor failed, things were playing out as Don Schneider had planned. His vision of a company with a large, national footprint and the determination to meet a broader and more complex set of customer needs while fighting relentlessly for market share was coming into sharper focus.

While many trucking companies failed to master this new competitive world, Schneider thrived in it and grew steadily. In a period of just over a quarter-century, the company evolved from a largely point-to-point carrier to one with a breadth of operations in intermodal, logistics, dedicated and international transportation. Over time, Schneider could provide whatever customers needed to move goods around in an increasingly global marketplace, becoming an essential backbone in its customers' supply chains. Meanwhile, the company grew more sophisticated in managing its numbers, its operations and even its culture in pursuit of a strategy to succeed in the present and ensure long-term sustainability.

Since deregulation, Schneider has turned its original business model on its head to survive — one might say lead — a transition in which shippers' needs and options changed dramatically. It became one of the few traditional trucking companies nimble and innovative enough to offer its customers the right combination of service and value while operating effectively in a deregulated market.

To do so, Schneider recast itself as an essentially union-free company. It moved from family to professional team management, all the while preserving its long-held values. It continually wielded technology as a competitive advantage, shifted from an exclusively long-haul company to a balanced long-haul and regional carrier, and set up an intermodal operation and then converted its business model. It put in place a structure and a form of governance designed to achieve Don's intentions that Schneider be successful after he was gone. Finally, consistent with its "leap of faith" mind-set, Schneider made a series of large capital investments in the teeth of the worst U.S. recession since the 1930s.

"It's hard to fathom that company and industry business models had to change so dramatically in such a short period of time in order for us to survive," says

A white trailer sits loaded with freight for a customer of Schneider's Dedicated division, which manages fleet operations for the businesses it serves. The customer requested the trailer's color when Schneider signed the contract.

To those unfamiliar with what makes Schneider tick, the company's orange trucks are its most familiar symbol, but Schneider has become much more than a trucking company. Don Schneider realized the importance of information technology early on, and the company's data center, above, is the "brain" that supports the myriad nodes that drive the business today.

Tom Vandenberg. "That we met the challenges head-on and survived is a testament to Don's determination to be successful, to the fortitude of the Schneider family and the faith they had in this organization and its people. It says a lot about our core values."

For customers, deregulation meant a major change in the way they went about their business. They now had more options available to them and were searching for carriers that could deliver speed, timeliness, precision and reliability in delivery, a broader array of services and the capacity to come up with unique solutions to complex and interrelated transportation problems. Kimberly-Clark (K-C) was so concerned about these issues that, in

anticipation of deregulation, it set up its own in-house trucking fleet in the mid-1970s as a hedge against any disruption in service. According to Kimberly-Clark Vice President Steven A. Harmon, the company outsourced some long-haul work to Schneider during that time and found Schneider so service-oriented by the 1980s that K-C handed Schneider more and more of its business.

Harmon says that by the 1990s, Schneider "had gotten so good at executing service at a competitive price value that we discontinued our fleet" and gave the work to Schneider in the largest private fleet conversion in Schneider's history. Today, Schneider provides a comprehensive set of transportation management services for K-C, from logistics planning to long-haul and intermodal freight delivery.

Schneider's ability to quickly adapt to changing conditions made the company extremely useful to its customers, according to Michelle Livingstone, vice president of transportation at The Home Depot, who also worked with Schneider when she was at JCPenney and Kraft Foods.

"Don Schneider always operated with integrity, and he was willing to do whatever he needed to do in order to meet his customers' needs," says Livingstone, who uses Schneider at The Home Depot for a variety of services, including dedicated, intermodal and one-way shipping. "My relationship with Schneider is not just transactional. They are really collaborative. They have top-notch engineering and analytics, and they come up with really innovative solutions to our challenges."

RESHAPING THE WORKFORCE

Schneider remained partly a union carrier after deregulation, in 1985 forming Schneider National Carriers (SNC) as an umbrella for all of its formerly separate union-free subsidiaries and restricting unionized operations to the Schneider Transport unit. Schneider did not abandon the older Transport side of the business, but it was increasingly committed to its union-free operations.

Although it had been years since the Teamsters' last work stoppage at Schneider (in 1982, against the Bulk division), the union hardly went away. For many years, believing it could turn drivers against Schneider, the union threatened to expel Schneider's union drivers from the Teamsters' pension plan unless the company added more union drivers. "The threats accelerated," Vandenberg says, "but the company's position was simple: if the union wanted more members, it needed to convince the existing nonunion drivers to vote for the union."

Then, in the mid-1990s, the Teamsters attempted to ratchet up the pressure from within by making good on its threats and kicking Schneider's union drivers out of the union pension fund as well as its health plan. That subjected Schneider to millions of dollars in withdrawal-liability penalties, inflicting pain on the company as well as on its drivers. Though the drivers were entitled to keep vested pension benefits, expulsion from the pension plan prevented them from accruing additional benefits. The impact was greatest on union drivers who were nearing landmarks of tenure, as they were denied step-level increases in benefits that would have been granted as they achieved milestones such as 10- or 20-year anniversaries with the company.

The union's gamble backfired. In response, Schneider proposed that the company exit the Teamsters' pension fund altogether and cover its drivers with a company-sponsored plan that provided drivers with the same benefits they would have received had they remained in the Teamsters' fund. It didn't help the union's cause that its pension plan, hobbled from the aftereffects of deregulation, was deteriorating financially. Rather than revolt and pressure the company to accede to union demands, Schneider's drivers cast their fate with the company over the union, continuing to work for and with Schneider. Predictably, the union resisted Schneider's proposal, and litigation dragged on for years. In the end, changing times wrung the life out of the Teamsters' pension plan, and it all but succumbed when the dot-com bubble burst in 2002. The following year, Schneider was finally and irrevocably free of the Teamsters' pension plan.

Vandenberg notes that in the years since deregulation, "virtually all Teamsters full-truckload companies evaporated, upending their drivers' work and retirement plans. The Schneider organization survived and succeeded in getting the vast majority of its Teamsters drivers to retirement on *their* schedule with full benefits.

Schneider drivers use a revolutionary, in-cab communications device called OmniTRACS to share load status and delivery information with the company's customer service team. The technology replaced a cumbersome, decades-old process in which drivers used pay phones to share information about their loads and receive assignments, and Schneider's customer service team used pen and paper for dispatch and tracking.

Continuity for the Long Haul

For Don Schneider, philosophy and business were inseparable.

A firm believer in the essential dignity of work, he felt that if Schneider were a well-run and efficient company, it would simultaneously serve customers, help keep the cost of goods low and contribute to a rising standard of living for people. It was therefore important to him that Schneider exist as long as it could as an independent company — one that could make solid business decisions consistent with the values that he and his family had ingrained in the company.

"Don operated at a higher level than most people," says Thomas Gannon, a key family advisor who served as the company's chief financial officer in the 1980s and '90s. "Don believed that in the process of building a better trucking company, we would also develop our people as more complete human beings and that their sense of self-worth and purpose would be enhanced."

While Don was leading the company through the great transformation that followed deregulation, he was also making significant changes, largely invisible to the outside world, to ensure the company's long-term survival.

Because he valued independence as the best way to meet evolving customer needs, Don wanted to structure ownership to enable Schneider to remain privately held in the future if that was how

the company could be most effective. He was fully aware, however, that private ownership had a potential downside: family disagreements and estate tax issues could create uncertainty and vulnerability. For those reasons, he took a series of actions over a span of about 10 years to improve the chances that the company would sustain itself well into the next generation.

Don began thinking about the future well before Al Schneider's death in 1983, and one thing he knew was that you couldn't run an effective company by committee. Consequently, after Al died and ownership of the company was shared by Don and his siblings, Don set out to consolidate ownership and leadership. By September 1984, he had acquired 54 percent of the company's stock and developed a plan to gain control of the remainder. There now was a clear leader who could provide unambiguous direction.

He then took steps to address governance. Don was determined that management, including himself, be as accountable to the health and growth of the business as if the company were publicly held. He concluded that Schneider and its stakeholders would be best served by an independent and robust board of directors that included people from outside the organization.

By 1990, he had established that board, including leaders from a mix of private and public

companies. Importantly, for objectivity and to ensure that family goals didn't impede good business decisions, Don structured the board so independent directors would always outnumber insiders. The only member of management that sits on the board of directors is the president of the corporation, and there are only two family members on the board. The remaining directors — currently six people — are independent, "at large" members.

At Don's urging, the board adopted strong bylaws on governance, addressing such things as conflicts of interest, director compensation, committee makeup and voting rights. An important consideration was the establishment of qualifications and tenure limits for directors. The board set an initial 12-year limit on board membership. As Gannon explains, "After 12 years, you've shared a lot of wisdom, and if the board is going to sustain itself, you need a combination of people who've been there a long time, some newcomers with a fresh perspective and some people in between."

Careful attention also was given to providing for director succession, given the critical role that the at-large directors played as both custodians of governance and representatives of shareholders. "Don knew that he could not foresee every future challenge that the company would face," Gannon says. "So he put an ownership and governance structure in place that relied on the experience and wisdom of the independent directors to make decisions in the best interests of his family and the company."

In a series of three transactions beginning in 1991, Don gifted the majority of his shares in the company into three trusts. In doing so, he paid millions of dollars in gift taxes he otherwise would not have owed until his death and surrendered much of his control over the company's destiny. While the trusts were set up with family members as beneficiaries, the at-large directors were named

as the voting trustees. By 1995, Don controlled no votes as a shareholder, and since he had only one of many votes on the board, he effectively had relinquished control of the company to which he had devoted his life's work.

Scott Trumbull, an independent director and the former non-executive chairman of Schneider's board, says the ownership and governance structures Don set up gave management the ability to objectively stay focused on the business and the flexibility to reshape the company in response

to market challenges. He says they also helped Schneider preserve Don's philosophy about the higher purposes of work.

"Don frequently reinforced the importance of our core values to the company's long-term success," Trumbull says. "As directors and trustees, we are humbled by the responsibility he entrusted to each of us to ensure that the company remains built to last."

In August 1995, in a move to keep Schneider National privately owned, Don Schneider established the second of three trusts into which he eventually put all his shares of company stock. He then named Schneider's outside board members as the voting trustees, ensuring that the company would be managed separately from the personal interests of family-member owners. At left is the certificate committing about a third of Don's shares to the 1995 trust.

Thomas Gannon helped Don Schneider recapitalize and restructure the company in 1984 in anticipation of a vastly changing future in the trucking industry. Gannon was Schneider's director of taxes at the time, and he went on to become chief financial officer and, later, a key liaison between the company and the Schneider family.

The company had kept the faith in and for its drivers against long odds."

CLEAR LEADERSHIP AND DIRECTION

Don Schneider was preoccupied with the events of the moment as Schneider navigated its way through early deregulation, but he also had been giving plenty of thought to the future of the company. He knew from watching his father that a successful operation couldn't be run by committee, and he suspected that Schneider would have to grow beyond him or the family if it wanted to remain in business. He also believed that involving multiple family members in key decisions had the potential to introduce conflicts of interest and that those had to be avoided if decisions were going to be made in the best interests of the company rather than of family members.

To prepare Schneider for what he saw as the trucking industry's future, Don had to change how the company was managed, and that began with ownership. When Al Schneider died, company stock had been placed in two trusts for the benefit of Al's wife, Agnes, and their children. The provisions gave each of Al's children a substantial ownership interest in the company. Don had

the largest share because he had acquired additional stock during his tenure with the company, which was longer than that of any of his siblings.

In 1984, Don worked with Dudley Godfrey from the Milwaukee law firm of Godfrey & Kahn, and Thomas Gannon, then director of taxes but later the company's chief financial officer, to recapitalize Schneider and restructure its ownership. His aim was to establish a strong and nimble company, based on his belief that an organization could not be managed effectively with fragmented ownership. Someone had to be in clear control. With Godfrey's assistance, the trusts were unwound and, with Gannon managing the financial and family negotiation complexities, the company redeemed enough shares to put a majority of the shares under the control of Don and his immediate family. Don's siblings owned most of the rest, and a small balance was in the hands of other members of management.

Within six years, Don's brothers Paul and Jim left day-to-day involvement in the business (brother David had departed back in 1963). Paul left in January 1986, having built the Bulk operation into a $50 million business; however, he was worn out by years of 80-hour workweeks and wave after wave of union negotiations. Jim Schneider stayed until 1990, when he resigned. He had been running Schneider's express transcontinental business, and he had significantly grown the operation and enjoyed doing so under Schneider Transport President Ed Thompson. But after 10 years at Schneider, Thompson left the company in 1987 to start a consulting business, and there was no chemistry between Jim Schneider and Thompson's successor, Jim Olson. Olson, who had joined Schneider as chief financial officer in 1985, brought the rigor to corporate finance that Don Schneider had sought, though he didn't have the people skills that had made Thompson both collegial and effective.

With Toronto's famous CN Tower in the background, a Schneider truck moves toward its destination. Schneider became an international operation in 1989 when it obtained authority to haul in several Canadian provinces.

Ernie Micek, below, and
Ed Powers, opposite,
were the first two outside
members of Schneider's
new board of directors
when it was formed in
1986. Don Schneider
recruited them for their
expertise and independent
thinking. At the time, Micek
was a senior executive with
Cargill, the nation's largest
privately held company,
and Powers was chairman
and CEO of The Mueller
Company.

Now in his 50s, Don became increasingly aware of
his own mortality when, during a routine physical,
doctors discovered a blocked coronary artery. His
wife, Pat, had always worried about the intensity with
which Don approached every aspect of life and about
his inability to relax. After Don underwent successful
angioplasty, he began to take his health more seriously.
He modified his diet, became a devoted runner and
experimented with various meditation techniques. Still,
he could sense the clock ticking.

One afternoon in 1986, Don called Gannon,
with whom he had grown close over the course of
negotiations with the family, into his office. Recognizing
the importance to the company of long-term continuity
in governance and management, he said, "Someday I'll
be like my dad — a guy who's been in the business a
long time and who thinks he knows everything, and, of
course, I won't know everything. I'm not going to want
to leave, and I need somebody who will tell me when it's
time to go. I need a board of directors."

It was important to Don that the board have heavy
representation from outside the Schneider family —
as outside members wouldn't feel any obligation to
make decisions based on assumed family agendas but
rather on adherence to Don's desires that the company
be run effectively. The first two board members that
Don recruited were Ernie Micek, a senior executive at
multinational food processor Cargill, and Ed Powers,
then chairman and chief executive officer of The Mueller
Company, a privately held manufacturer of water
distribution products. At the time, Cargill was the world's
largest privately held company, so Micek was very
familiar with the demands on professional management
in a family-owned organization.

Don took his time selecting the rest of the board.
He interviewed every candidate at length and devoted
more than a year to assembling the group he wanted.

While the search was on, Micek chaired a governance
committee and, working with Don and Gannon, began
to define and encode the tenets of the board. Ultimately
an eight-member board was in place, with the majority
of the members independent ("at-large") directors.
Bylaws restricted family membership to just two slots,
and strict guidelines were adopted for succession, with
term limits (12 years) and a mandatory retirement age
(initially 68) to keep the board fresh and vital but with
continuity over time. Pay was based on attendance,
not membership.

"What I found unusual was how Don instilled his
core values in the company," Micek recalls. "A trucking
company tends to have a lot of turnover, but Don drove
the values into the business. At almost every meeting of
the board, he'd make a little speech and he would direct

it especially at his executive team. He'd say, 'We have to do better than our competition. If we can't deliver better value, we don't deserve the business.'"

THE BRIGHT BLADE OF TECHNOLOGY

With ownership simplified and a new form of governance in place, Don was ready to advance toward the future with the same steely confidence he'd displayed through the first years of deregulation. The saber he would brandish this time was the bright blade of technology.

Don knew technology would become central to his business and he believed it would reshape the entire industry, setting off a cascade of new capabilities that would lead to new services. Those services, in turn, would create a demand for new kinds of information, which would in turn make possible faster, more accurate, more complex and more data-driven processes and decisions. Enabled in part by advances in technology, Don believed, the logistics business would evolve to support the emergence of just-in-time manufacturing and the related importance of regional distribution networks. In the bargain, he thought, the ancient struggle between railroads and trucking would have to give way to mutually beneficial cooperation.

In 1987, when more trucking companies declared bankruptcy than in any year since deregulation, Schneider was operating almost 2,500 tractors and 9,100 trailers, not including owner-operators. It was about to buy 1,200 additional tractors — better than past models, with 110-inch sleepers that allowed drivers to get better rest. That investment, though large, was small compared to the next big investment Schneider was about to make.

At about the same time that Don Schneider and Wayne Lubner had first visited Seville, Ohio, to scout the operating center site, University of California-San Diego professor Irwin Jacobs was hosting a meeting at his home that would lead to the creation of Qualcomm, which

would become a leading provider of wireless technology. Qualcomm's first product was a tracking and messaging service, three years in development, called OmniTRACS. Supported by satellite technology, it was built specifically for the trucking industry.

"Everyone was skeptical that we could have a very small device that fits on a truck be low-cost and yet work over satellites designed for very large terminals," Jacobs reflected as he looked back on the development of OmniTRACS 20 years later. "We managed to achieve that."

When Don Schneider signed a contract with Qualcomm to adapt OmniTRACS for his entire fleet in 1988, it was every bit as much a leap of faith as any of those previously taken by Don or his father. Schneider was Qualcomm's first, largest — in fact, only — customer at the time it signed the contract, and there wasn't even a production model to look at. "It was a brave and bold decision," says Jacobs. "Qualcomm was an unproven company, and it was unproven technology."

This was no small risk for Schneider to take. The company wasn't just upgrading its computer or communications network; it was adopting a comprehensive fleet management system that would require a large financial investment coupled with substantial changes in the way Schneider people went about their work and in the commitments they made and services they provided to customers.

Schneider installed OmniTRACS on 5,000 trucks. The initial investment cost the company a whopping $26 million, but it proved to be worth it. Schneider became the first trucking company capable of sending and receiving messages directly between drivers and company computers. Communication time between drivers and dispatchers was shaved to virtually zero, and the frustrating days of drivers calling in on phone banks were over. Furthermore, Schneider modified its

Green Pumpkins

Schneider National was committed to "green" transportation decades before the word green took on its now popular connotation of environmental responsibility. In 1978, the company launched an engineering program to enhance the aerodynamic efficiency of tractors, converted the fleet to cost-saving radial tires and began training drivers about how to use less fuel on the road.

The impact of those programs is quantifiable. Since 1978, energy efficiency initiatives have saved tens of millions of gallons of diesel fuel every year. At the same time, these initiatives have reduced carbon dioxide emissions by 1.2 billion pounds per year, particulate matter by more than 350 tons and nitrous oxide by 10,226 tons.

In the ensuing 30 years, Schneider has remained a pioneer in green transportation. In 1985, it introduced driver incentives for idle reduction and fuel management. Six years later, it implemented highly efficient intermodal service. In 1995, Schneider National Bulk Carriers became a partner of Responsible Care, a global initiative developed by the chemical industry to improve health, safety and environmental performance. In 2003, Schneider was the first major truckload carrier to outfit company trucks with no-idle heaters, further reducing emissions.

A charter member of the SmartWay Transportation Partnership — a U.S. Environmental Protection Agency program that helps freight companies improve fuel efficiency, increase environmental performance and increase supply-chain sustainability — Schneider has been recognized repeatedly with the SmartWay Award of Excellence.

Modern Freightliner tractors, like the 25,000th truck delivered to Schneider in 2013, employ state-of-the-art engines, transmissions and aerodynamic design to achieve significant gains in fuel efficiency over models introduced in 2010, the year in which *Fleet Owner* magazine named Schneider its Green Fleet of the Year.

Schneider operates one of the most energy-efficient fleets on the road today, having employed aerodynamic features such as wheel covers and side skirts to become a pioneer in reducing fuel consumption for 40 years. Opposite, the 25,000th Freightliner truck delivered to Schneider.

The boatload of orange containers aboard a Danish cargo ship, right, makes a bold statement about Schneider's commitment to intermodal transportation. The boxes don't contain cargo yet, as they're brand new, acquired by Schneider as part of a multimillion dollar conversion of the intermodal operation begun in 2008. Railroads, challenged by skyrocketing West Coast imports from Asia and limited by track capacity, demanded that trucking companies increase their use of stackable, container-on-flat-car (COFC) boxes, as on the train opposite.

SOURCE system so dispatchers, in real time, could learn the whereabouts of trucks and trailers and the way they were being operated. Service to customers improved, and in the first year after installation, OmniTRACS made Schneider so much more efficient that empty mileage was slashed by 25 percent. The company's adoption of OmniTRACS ignited a transformation that would soon overtake the industry.

GOING INTERMODAL

By the early 1990s, innovative technology was becoming evident in every corner of the Schneider world. The company's investment in Qualcomm had set the stage for many other changes that would have been impossible without the benefits in speed, information sharing and quality that cutting-edge technology enabled. Even before the installation of OmniTRACS, Schneider was becoming a sophisticated manager of supply-chain logistics, but OmniTRACS made it easier for Schneider to get better at logistics, and that in turn facilitated another leap of faith in 1991.

The days of railroads' dominance in freight transport were long gone, but some trucking companies had discovered that it was possible to achieve significant efficiencies by collaborating rather than competing with railroads. That November, in support of its long-haul trucking model, Schneider joined them — making its entrée into intermodal transport with an agreement with the Southern Pacific Railroad to serve routes between California and the Midwest.

Schneider called its intermodal operation TruckRail, and it was developed under the leadership of Woody Richardson and Todd Jadin. Richardson, a 10-year veteran of the company at the time and a University of Wisconsin-Madison graduate who also had earned a master's degree in civil engineering and transportation from the Massachusetts Institute of Technology, had

been an operations analyst for the Burlington Northern Railroad before joining Schneider. "I knew something about railroads," he says with a shrug, "and Craig Philip, who was vice president of Southern Pacific's intermodal division at the time, was a classmate of mine at MIT."

Intermodal was so new that companies competing in that business were inventing it on the fly. Furthermore, nobody got into intermodal on the cheap, and to make its partnership with Southern Pacific feasible, Schneider invested a small fortune in a fleet of Southern Pacific Domestic Unit (SPDU, or "spud") containers specifically designed for use on railroad flat cars.

Jadin, who had joined Schneider in 1985 to provide customer and driver support, set up major market hubs for dray as the company made a serious intermodal commitment. Schneider completed the Southern Pacific hub in Chicago, off Interstate 55, in November 1991, and Jadin quickly established additional TruckRail

Truck driving is not a career for everyone, but it offers special benefits for those who decide to climb behind the wheel of a big rig. One of those perks, many Schneider drivers will tell you, is the opportunity to see the varied and often breathtakingly beautiful landscapes of America, such as this tidal marsh on the coast of Georgia.

Wielding a Qualcomm device as though it were a *Star Wars* weapon, Don Schneider posed for the dramatic photo in the February 1992 *Fortune* magazine, below. The related feature story profiled Don and four other innovative business leaders dubbed the "New Revolutionaries" for the way they had shaken up their industries. Opposite, the immense customer service center at Schneider's world headquarters in Green Bay covers an acre. Hundreds of customer service personnel and dispatchers keep freight loads on track and on time around the clock.

centers in northern and southern California, Portland, Atlanta and Memphis as Schneider signed agreements with the Santa Fe, Burlington Northern, Union Pacific, Norfolk Southern, Wisconsin Central, Florida East Coast, Canadian National, Canadian Pacific, Illinois Central and Conrail systems. Within a year, Schneider was able to ship freight intermodally to almost any major market in North America.

THE NEW REVOLUTIONARY

Expanding quickly in the newly competitive industry, by 1991 Schneider had outgrown its headquarters at 2777 South Ridge Road in Green Bay, where it employed about 900 people. With projections that employment would reach 1,500 by mid-decade, the company announced plans for a new, $15 million, 220,000-square-foot customer service and corporate business center in Ashwaubenon, a Green Bay suburb. By 1992, the company had reached $1 billion in annual revenue and was attracting widespread attention for its innovative use of information technology. *Fortune* magazine profiled Don Schneider among five innovative business leaders in February that year, photographing him wearing trucker's coveralls and leaping from a Schneider cab, clutching a Qualcomm device in one hand. The headline: "MEET THE NEW REVOLUTIONARIES."

"When you see today that every truck in industry-leading Schneider National's fleet has sprouted a jaunty little satellite antenna, when you look in the cab and see ... an 'associate'

FEBRUARY 24, 1992

FORTUNE

MANAGING

MEET THE NEW REVOLUTIONARIES

Five hot companies shut out competitors by rewriting the rules of their industries. How they did so holds valuable strategic lessons for any manager.   ■ *by Myron Magnet*

Schneider National CEO Don Schneider took a flying leap into the future and triumphed. Competitors—those that are still around—are following at last.

PHOTOGRAPHS BY PETER SIBBALD

with a merit pay plan and an onboard computer that links him to headquarters — you know you're looking at a whole new species," author Myron Magnet wrote.

Don personified that new species. A decidedly conservative man who, like his father, had spent his career wearing suits and ties, he began to show up at the office dressed in blue jeans, denim shirts and cowboy boots. The western garb seemed an apt symbol of the transformation that Schneider National was leading. In the post-deregulation environment, the staid, pick-it-up-and-drop-it-off business had become the Wild West, and who better to scout a trail through it than a man who dressed like John Wayne?

Further underscoring the commitment Schneider was making to a technologically driven future, the upstart technology and culture magazine *Wired* declared Schneider National to be "an information company masquerading as a trucking line." No wonder. In the five years after Schneider took a calculated risk with Qualcomm, the company's revenues had doubled. Now, in back rooms, "rat packs" of engineers and programmers wrestled with the business problems of some of Schneider's largest customers.

SCHNEIDER ENTERS LOGISTICS

What really distinguished Don Schneider from other industry leaders was his vision. One of the reasons he was so dedicated to technology was because he foresaw that the future of transportation lay not just in *doing* it but also in *managing* it. When the company's new headquarters

Wherever Procter & Gamble or any other Schneider customer needs to move its products, Schneider makes sure they get there on time and on budget.

opened, its offices were wrapped around an atrium that sprawled over an acre. There, hundreds of customer service personnel and dispatchers — linked by phones and computers — would collaborate to develop the most cost-effective and efficient pathway for freight, for every customer, every delivery, every day. Since 1992, this place, which associates often refer to as "mission control," has been a hive of frenetic activity, buzzing around the clock, seven days a week.

By 1993, Schneider could move any kind of freight worldwide by truck, train or ship, and it had the capacity to track shipments quickly and efficiently with pinpoint precision. Taking advantage of these new capabilities, customers developed increasingly complex shipping requirements and turned more and more to vendors like Schneider to provide integrated solutions to meet them.

Schneider had mastered logistics in order to better serve its existing customers, but in the process, it had developed a skill set that could be marketed on its own. Even though established firms had been providing

logistics services to many leading corporations for several years, Don and his management team were convinced that Schneider could compete with them. In January 1993, again following Don's instincts and belief in his people, they put that conviction to the test, forming Schneider Logistics Inc. to provide a spectrum of services, from single-source transportation management involving carrier selection and control functions to comprehensive logistics management.

Larry Sur, who had guided development of many of the technological innovations that made Schneider's preeminence in the field possible, was named president of the new division. Keenly focused on using technology as an advantage, he bolstered his staff by hiring a new vice president of engineering and systems, Chris Lofgren. With a master's degree in industrial and management systems engineering and a doctorate in industrial and systems engineering, Lofgren had worked for Symantec Corporation, Motorola and CAPS Logistics. Though bright and capable and possessing solid credentials, there was nothing about him on the day he arrived at Schneider that would suggest the role he would play in the company's future.

So adept was Schneider Logistics that on March 14, 1994, it was awarded a contract worth hundreds of millions of dollars to manage the shipment of all 435,000 parts that General Motors sent to dealers, warehouse distributors and mass merchandisers *every day*. Not only was it a huge coup for Schneider Logistics, it was the largest logistics contract ever awarded. To win the business, Schneider bested two of the nation's most capable logistics firms: Caliber of Akron, Ohio, and Menlo of San Mateo, California.

"We reengineered all of [General Motors'] dealer deliveries and made extensive improvements in their delivery network and service levels [and] saved them over 10 percent on their freight costs," says Sur.

Reorganizing the GM operation took 18 months.

Landing the GM contract was a signal achievement, but it wasn't the only big fish the company netted. After two months of intensive planning, Schneider Dedicated took over Kimberly-Clark's fleet of 550 tractors. It was Schneider's largest private fleet conversion ever, and during the first week of July 1994, Schneider trucks delivered more than 1,000 Kimberly-Clark loads with a 99 percent on-time record. A similar distribution and logistics contract was soon inked with Scott Paper.

In a rapidly globalizing marketplace, it was essential that a firm in the logistics business have an international presence. Schneider had first become an international company in 1989, when, a year after the signing of a free-trade agreement between the United States and Canada, the company obtained authority to haul in the Canadian provinces of Quebec, Ontario and British Columbia. By 1994, the North American Free Trade Agreement had supplanted that earlier agreement, and the entire continent was on its way to becoming one large, integrated marketplace.

Schneider responded to its customers' increasing North American needs by purchasing a small Mexican carrier, Transpo Virel, in mid-1993. Mexico's state-owned railroad company, Ferrocarriles Nacionales de México (FNDM), then invited Schneider to discuss a cross-border intermodal relationship. Todd Jadin accepted FNDM's invitation, and the meeting went so well that he got a 90-day assignment to remain in Mexico and work out the details. Almost as soon as he arrived, the collapse of the Salinas government caused a significant devaluation of the peso. Jadin's 90-day project turned into a long-term assignment, and he spent two years restructuring Schneider's investment. Then, as vice president of Schneider's Mexico division, he grew the company's international and domestic Mexico business from $20 million to $150 million.

ALL-IN ON TECHNOLOGY

In repositioning the company to meet the new realities of its industry, Don Schneider concluded that some operations didn't serve the core mission or were consuming resources that were needed to grow the business elsewhere. Chief among them was Schneider Communications, which by 1995 had become Wisconsin's leading communications company, with nearly 11,000 business customers. In August 1995, Schneider sold the unit to Frontier Corporation of Rochester, New York — helping to make Frontier the nation's fifth largest long-distance company.

Don Detampel, a Schneider veteran and president of Schneider Communications, says Schneider had reached a critical juncture where it either needed to invest heavily in technology or get out of the communications business. With some reluctance, Don Schneider chose the latter. "As we got into the 1990s," Detampel recalls, "the phone business was changing, and we wondered if we had the scale to compete."

In 1995, a year in which Schneider surpassed $2 billion in revenue for the first time, two people of note departed the Schneider fold: Al's wife, Agnes, passed away after a long battle with Alzheimer's disease, and Jim Olson resigned as president of Schneider after 10 years. The death of Agnes — widow of the founder and undeniably the mother of the company in nearly 50 years at her husband's side — made the gulf between simpler times and the present industry juggernaut seem wider than ever.

Olson was succeeded by former Coast Guard officer John Lanigan, who had joined Schneider in 1984 and served five years as vice president and general manager of Dedicated. By 1995, Schneider had absorbed more than 90 other companies' fleets. Dedicated soon entered the refrigerated business by converting the Anchor Express fleet — more than 130 refrigerated trailers — for

Anchor Foods, a large food products company. That set the stage for a refrigerated business that today serves the likes of Walmart.

Meanwhile, Don Schneider continued his "all-in" march in technology. In January 1997, he and Lofgren, who had been named the company's CIO the previous autumn, formed a steering committee charged with finding ways to use emerging technologies to improve business performance. One of the first products to emerge was Schneider Track and Trace (STAT), the company's first Web-based application. It enabled customers to check the location and status of their freight online around the clock. The technological enhancements made Schneider more efficient and effective, spurring business growth, which in turn pushed the company to further invest in technology to make the entire business perform even better.

Technology was not the only major investment Schneider made at the time. With the industry mired in a prolonged nationwide driver shortage, Schneider fortified its core business by purchasing four trucking companies in 1998. Although the acquisitions brought the company new customers, the primary motive was to add drivers. Schneider acquired Iowa-based Highway Carrier Corporation in the spring, followed by Builders Transport, based in South Carolina, and Alabama-based Landstar Poole within two weeks of each other in the summer. Finally, Schneider added Tennessee-based A. J. Metler Hauling and Rigging to grow its Specialized division's glass and flatbed capacity later in the year.

Companywide, business was booming. In just four years, the Dedicated fleet had more than doubled, from 3,000 to 6,470 trucks. In contrast, Miami-based Ryder had grown its dedicated fleet by less than 15 percent over the same period. Schneider was also breathing down Ryder's neck in logistics: the roster of leading corporations turning to Schneider for logistics support

The $26 million contract Don Schneider signed with Qualcomm in 1988 was one of the many leaps of faith that helped Schneider outpace the competition over the years. The efficiency that Qualcomm's technology, above and in the cab opposite, brought to the supply chain was game-changing in the transportation industry and gave Schneider a competitive advantage for years.

now included GM, Ford, Chrysler, Case, PPG Industries, Thomson Consumer Electronics, Simpson Paper Company and Scott Paper.

In October 1998, a *Transport Topics* feature lauded Schneider's technical capabilities, noting the innovations Schneider systems engineers had developed to enhance logistics management, including SUMIT (Schneider Utility for Managing Integrated Transportation), a shipment control system that incorporates all facets of the shipment cycle; SSP (Schneider Shipment Planner), a carrier selection and shipment consolidation system; and STAT.

SACRIFICING POWER AND CONTROL

As Schneider continued to expand its footprint, add to its services and improve operations, behind the scenes, Don was working determinedly to create an ownership structure that would allow the company to remain

private if the board of directors concluded that doing so was in the best interest of the company and all its constituents. Understanding the challenges that estate tax law presented to that goal, he was willing to surrender a large amount of his personal control and sacrifice a significant amount of money to achieve it.

Beginning that year, Don created three trusts (the second was set up in 1995, the third in 2000), and each time, he gifted about a third of his shares of Schneider stock into the trusts. Tax laws forced him to pay millions of dollars in gift taxes; the company lent him the money to pay the taxes, and Don repaid it over time. While Don's children were named as the trusts' beneficiaries, they were given no control; instead, to preserve continuity of ownership through multiple family branches and to prevent potential family-driven disruptions to the business, a voting trust agreement gave Schneider's at-large directors all voting rights for shares in the trusts. Don thus gave up nearly all of his own voting privileges, ensuring that those most responsible for the successful management of the business — the directors — had the greatest say in major decisions about the company's future.

Not long after the second trust was established, an ominous cloud appeared over Schneider's great success. For some time, Don Schneider had been growing forgetful. Ever since the blocked-artery incident, he had taken good care of himself, but by the late 1990s, he was in his mid-60s, and occasional forgetfulness was not uncommon for a man his age. The mental lapses grew more frequent, however, and then profound. Soon, Don was diagnosed with Alzheimer's disease, the incurable affliction from which his mother had suffered. He accepted the diagnosis with characteristic grace. There were things he wanted to accomplish, and he had a new sense of how little time he had left to accomplish them.

Thanks to Don's foresight, Schneider by now had

a well-functioning board of directors, and it was faced with the unenviable task of contemplating who Don's successor should be. "Don was passionately devoted to the continuity of ownership, governance and management," Gannon says. "It was critical that the board find the right person."

NAMING A SUCCESSOR

The ideal successor would have been a senior executive who had been in the business for many years, understood it and knew where Don wanted to take it. There were no obvious homegrown choices, but a few people who had begun their careers elsewhere were contenders.

Don Schneider thought highly of Don Detampel. Though Detampel had left Schneider in 1995 with the Schneider Communications sale, Don Schneider stayed in touch with him and on several occasions tried to lure him back to the company. "I was very close to Don," says Detampel. "I was tempted to come back. I loved the technology I worked on at Schneider, but in 1995 the technology bubble was just getting rolling, and I didn't have the same passion for trucking that I had for communications."

Another possibility was Lofgren, who was named chief operating officer (COO) of the company in 2000, succeeding the departing John Lanigan, whose career had risen with the tide of transformative technology.

Ironically, just as Lofgren became COO, the company announced its decision to spin off the division that perhaps best exemplified the value of technology — Schneider Logistics. The spinoff never took place, though, as the bubble of investor interest in Internet-related technology, three years in the making, burst the following spring. As the whistling balloon rapidly deflated, Schneider backed off on its decision. "The problem with Logistics was that we had no idea how to price it in order to make money," says Lofgren. With Lofgren's

leadership, Schneider soon solved that problem, and as the first decade of the new century played out, it became quickly apparent that keeping Logistics was the right move. Moreover, in the eyes of the board, there was a growing conviction that Lofgren was the man to take over from Don Schneider.

Fittingly, the board that had been put in place at Don's behest to tell him when it was time to go did just that — asking him to step down as CEO in the summer of 2002. While Don remained on the board, Lofgren was named the company's third president and CEO, and its first from outside the family. Explaining his appointment, Lofgren says with characteristic humility, "I was just the last man standing."

In truth, Lofgren was stepping into the boots of an icon. If it was a great honor, it was also a great challenge. "Chris was tasked with leading the company during another transition," says Steve Matheys, executive vice president and chief administrative officer, who joined Schneider in 1994 and held leadership roles in IT before succeeding Lofgren as CIO in 2000. "The company had back-to-back family leaders, and now it was moving away from that model to a professional management team and an external board."

It was a revolutionary change, but it was not as though Schneider was inexperienced in that respect. Furthermore, Don had not gone away. He was still there if the new president wanted his opinion, but he didn't intrude where he wasn't invited. He'd stop by to see Lofgren and ask him, "How you doing? You getting exercise? Eating right?" Otherwise, he trusted that Lofgren was up to the task, and he left the new man to work things out for himself.

THE VALUE TRIANGLE

Lofgren began working things out immediately. In no hurry to install his own leadership team and eager

Chris Lofgren, left, poses with Don Schneider, the man he succeeded as president of Schneider National.

Chris Lofgren championed The Value Triangle, a pragmatic business strategy with three legs: hiring outstanding drivers and treating them well, providing excellent service to customers and generating profits that can be reinvested in Schneider's future. Recognizing that very little can remain static in a world where change is constant and rapid, Lofgren has nevertheless been steadfast in his devotion to Schneider's core values, established more than 75 years ago.

to maintain continuity, Lofgren moved quickly on other fronts, working with the team he had inherited from Don to re-engineer the company's fundamental business processes — knowing that the flexibility to succeed in constantly evolving markets demanded operations of the utmost efficiency. Called The Process Journey, the re-engineering initiative aimed to redefine everything Schneider does — from pursuing new business to developing solutions to processing customers' transportation orders to delivering freight — from the customer's point of view.

"Chris and the leadership team identified that Schneider, as a company, was in the wrong place," says Matheys. "We no longer could be just a long-haul transportation company. We needed to be strong regionally. We had a great opportunity in the dray space, where intermodal and trucking intersect. We were not equipped to do everything in the international market, but if we focused on doing what we do best, we could be a force to be contended with in other countries, like cross-border Mexico and Canada and domestic China."

Well before deregulation, American businesses had begun experimenting with just-in-time manufacturing. With fewer and fewer warehouses, products were being assembled and delivered with precision unimaginable in the early days of long haul.

"Our customers were building regional networks, and by the early 2000s, long-haul business was shrinking about 10 percent a year," says Lofgren. Moreover, much of the long-haul volume was being handled intermodally. Once again, Schneider reinvented itself. No longer just a long-haul trucker, it became a multi-dimensional transportation business as comfortable with logistics management and intermodal freight delivery as it was with traditional trucking on any geographic scale.

It was in this context that the new CEO found himself increasingly in the role of uniting two previous — and

decidedly different — visions of the company. Founder Al Schneider had been a trucker; under him, Schneider was a trucking company, and Al's focus was on the drivers. Don, who went to business school, was a customer service man, and he put the attention on solving customers' problems, sometimes without full recognition of the cost. Lofgren saw these ways of managing the company as two legs of a triangle — each essential to Schneider's success but with one stabilizing leg missing: a focus on profits that could be reinvested in the company's future. "We were the fastest growing, the biggest, but we weren't always the most profitable company," Lofgren says.

Based on this thinking, in 2007 Lofgren and his team introduced The Value Triangle, a new approach that made equally substantial commitments to associates, customers and the business. Schneider was soon benchmarking best practices throughout the industry and sharing information with associates, and before long, it changed its organizational structure, aligning the company around revenue-generating business units rather than internal function. This gave leaders of the business units full accountability for revenue and expenses, direct management of the resources they needed and the authority to make decisions. The previous structure, Lofgren says, "didn't foster the evolution of business leaders."

WORLD WITHIN REACH

As Don Schneider had envisioned, the long-haul market shrank, supply chains moved increasingly closer to customers and the logistics business grew more important than ever. The company responded by continuing to build that part of its operation while making clear that it would exit a business not critical to Schneider's future.

In 2006, for example, the company sold Schneider Specialized Carriers, a specialist in heavy-haul and open-equipment transportation. Specialized had begun life as International Transport, but in 1990 it was transformed under the leadership of Mike Weiss, one of the young military officers Don Schneider had recruited in the 1970s. Don gave Weiss the autonomy to do what he thought was right for the business, and Weiss and his team responded with an innovative idea to expand the division to include the hauling of raw and architectural glass. The team collaborated with Indiana trailer manufacturer Wabash National to develop a flexible trailer — a flatbed that could open, butterfly fashion, to carry a load of glass one way and completely different products on the backhaul. Specialized flourished, becoming the largest glass carrier in the country by the mid-1990s. Ten years later, however, it was no longer critical to Schneider's core mission, and the company sold it.

Beginning that same year, one in which Schneider surpassed $3 billion in annual revenue, the company reinforced its Logistics business, with a focus on international capabilities. It acquired three small companies, with the result that Schneider became the first truckload carrier to offer door-to-door international logistics services. Logistics opened an office in Shanghai, China, in 2005 and began offering supply-chain consulting services.

In China, where comprehending the language often begins with understanding the meaning of words and names when their phonetic spelling is broken into constituent syllables, Schneider becomes "Shi Neng Da." It means "world within reach," an appropriate rallying cry for a giant international operation planting its flag nearly 7,000 miles from Green Bay, Wisconsin. By 2007, the company would be granted authority to operate as a domestic carrier and logistics services provider in China, a first among North American truckload providers. To service the new business, Schneider acquired the

operating assets of Bayoun Logistics, one of China's top 30 private logistics enterprises. Logistics further enlarged its global footprint in 2008 by setting up five new freight-forwarding locations, in Chicago, Atlanta, New York, Rotterdam and Amsterdam.

On another front, Schneider Intermodal was about to undergo a major transformation — in the middle of the most severe financial crisis in eight decades, no less.

"IT'S IN OUR DNA"

Late in 2007, as capital liquidity dried up in the wake of a collapse in the housing market the year before, the U.S. economy slumped to its knees, and by the middle of 2008, the resulting recession had swept around the world like a pandemic. It would turn out to be the worst financial disaster since the Great Depression, and it would drag on for three years, affecting businesses in every sector of the economy.

The trucking industry was not immune. Between

In the shadow of the Great Wall, two Schneider trucks speak to the company's international presence. With the world's second largest economy, China presents great long-haul opportunities for a company that cut its teeth on long-haul operations. Based in Tianjin, Schneider's China business is aggressively looking for opportunities to grow.

Living Orange

Green Bay Traffic Commission. Like everything else he became involved with, Don was wholly engaged with his charitable and community improvement activities, and those programs benefited from his capacity to recruit others. "I never saw Don when he wasn't driven," says Fox Valley businessman John F. Bergstrom, chairman and chief executive officer of the Bergstrom Corporation, who served with Don on the board of directors of the Green Bay Packers for two decades. "No matter what he turned his attention to, he was the consummate person trying to figure out a better way."

The genesis of the Schneider National Foundation was Don Schneider's abiding interest in physical fitness. A longtime jogger, he got the idea for an annual Schneider Run while participating in Green Bay's Bellin Run, a nationally renowned, 10-kilometer event sponsored by Bellin Memorial Hospital since 1977 to promote cardiovascular health.

For 25 years, Schneider's fitness event enjoyed strong support among associates. Don was determined that Schneider would continue to find a way to support health and give something back to the community where Schneider National had taken root and flourished.

In 1982, he created the Schneider National Foundation to support charitable and nonprofit organizations. While the initial focus of the foundation's largesse was on health and human services, its scope evolved to also cover arts and culture, children and education. In the years since it was launched, the foundation has donated tens of millions of dollars and hundreds of thousands of volunteer hours to an extraordinary range of charities, in Green Bay as well as in many other locations served by Schneider.

Don Schneider also served as chairman of the Capital Campaign for Notre Dame Academy, the United Way of Brown County's annual campaign and the Catholic High School Foundation. Don picked up his commitment to public service from his father, Al, who was a founding member of the Green Bay Packers Hall of Fame and a longtime member of the

Ask almost any Schneider associate who champions a cause, volunteers time or donates to an organization in need, and they'll say they give back because it's simply the right thing to do. They call it "Living Orange," a spirit of community stewardship that happens thousands of times each year in every community that Schneider calls home. It includes, clockwise from opposite, top, support for My Team Triumph (an organization that enables individuals with disabilities to participate in athletic events), a 25-year commitment to the Schneider Family Fitness event, a community art installation and a Habitat for Humanity house raising. Opposite, bottom, Vince Hagen, a U.S. Army veteran and driver of the 2008 Ride of Pride truck, places a wreath on a grave in Arlington National Cemetery as part of the annual Wreaths Across America program in 2012. Schneider also delivered nearly 10,000 wreaths to Fort Sam Houston National Cemetery in San Antonio that year.

The company now has seven Ride of Pride trucks in its fleet—an honor held only by Schneider National. The 2013 truck is driven by Chuck Ceccacci.

road truckload operation for most of its modern history, using the same fleet of trailers for both trucks and trains and relying on intermodal "for overflow capacity, as an alternative to trucking." A booming market in Asian imports challenged that model and forced the conversion of the Intermodal fleet, he says. "As the capacity on rail networks got tighter, the railroads had to move to a double-stack model," and that required a conversion from trailers to containers, Matheson says. "We had no choice but to convert."

And not much time. The conversion, begun in 2006, was completed in only three years, allowing Matheson, as president of Intermodal, to reshape the division with a more disciplined network optimized for serving Asian imports and, later, over-the-road conversion in Eastern markets as truck capacity became tighter. Consequently, Intermodal is one of the company's fastest-growing divisions.

A GREAT TESTAMENT

Don Schneider was 72 years old when, in 2007, he reached the mandatory retirement age stipulated in company bylaws and resigned from the board that he had so carefully constructed. He became chairman emeritus, a position he would hold for the rest of his life. The board held a private dinner for him, an opportunity to reminisce one last time about the things they had accomplished together under his leadership over almost three decades. Then Don stepped away from the company that had been his passion for most of his life.

Meanwhile, Lofgren began to put in place members of the management team that would move the company into the future. He had spent several years evaluating the talents and leadership styles of many people in the organization, and as changes took place with increasing speed in the industry in the late 2000s, he assigned new executives to roles in which they could lead the required

2007 and 2009, truckload volumes dropped by 20 percent, erasing a decade's worth of growth. More than 300,000 trucks were mothballed as some 6,700 trucking companies folded. As business contracted, Schneider was forced to trim its fleet of trucks by 11 percent, its ranks of drivers by 9 percent and its overall workforce by 9 percent. Even a setback as significant as that could not stand between Schneider and its destiny, however, and when Intermodal decided to convert from a trailer-on-flatcar (TOFC) to a container-on-flatcar operation, Schneider didn't hesitate. It invested $87 million to meet changes in that critical and growing market.

"We know where we want our business to go, and if we need to make investments to get there, we'll make them," says Lofgren. "It's in our DNA."

Bill Matheson, who joined Schneider in 1983, explains that Schneider had been primarily an over-the-evolution of their businesses. Mark Rourke, who had cut his teeth with Schneider as a service team leader at the Seville Operating Center, was named president of Truckload Services in 2006; if it moved by truck, it now reported to him. Matheson was named president of Intermodal in 2006, and in 2007, Judy Lemke joined Schneider as executive vice president and CIO after a long career with Medtronic, the world's largest medical technology company.

Lemke's charge was to transform Schneider from top to bottom, an extension of The Process Journey effort launched five years earlier. "This is a company that has a really good … understanding [of] the power, the limits and the implications of technology," she told a reporter for *WTN News* that spring, noting that it was no accident that both Lofgren and Matheys had previously served as CIO.

Lemke had been on the job fewer than six months when she announced that Oracle would help Schneider create a powerful new information platform to transform the enterprise for the foreseeable future. "Companies rely on Schneider to transport materials efficiently, prepare for seasonal and promotional spikes in volume, manage transportation services across continents and ensure that goods are moved out of ports as quickly and safely as possible," she said at the time. "We are embarking on this transformation to ensure that we continue to promote the success of our customers' operations … and keep their supply chains running as efficiently as possible."

The new initiative was called Quest, and by the time the conversion was completed in 2013, it would cost more than $250 million. Lofgren supports the investment, another large expenditure made in the midst of the Great Recession. "It's essential that we drive effectiveness across every area of the business," he says. "Considering the economic climate, most companies would have said,

'Let's wait on this,' but we're not afraid of risk. Even in the worst troughs of the economic cycle, if investments are necessary to ensure that Schneider is built to last, then we're prepared to make those investments."

The reinvention of the business that Lofgren had initiated was a monumental task, and it called for premium talent. In 2011, Lori Lutey came on board as chief financial officer following a 20-year career with FedEx that had included stints as a senior financial analyst, manager of sales finance and vice president of finance and administration for FedEx Supply Chain Services. Lofgren and his team were fortunate to have the strong support of LuEllen Oskey, director of executive administration since 2004. Oskey had begun her Schneider career in 1978, and she brought to the executive suite a wealth of experience in operations, customer service and human resources. Lofgren's

Technology plays such an important role in Schneider's success that three key leadership positions are held by people with IT backgrounds: left to right, Chris Lofgren, president and CEO; Steve Matheys, executive vice president and chief administrative officer; and Judy Lemke, executive vice president and chief information officer.

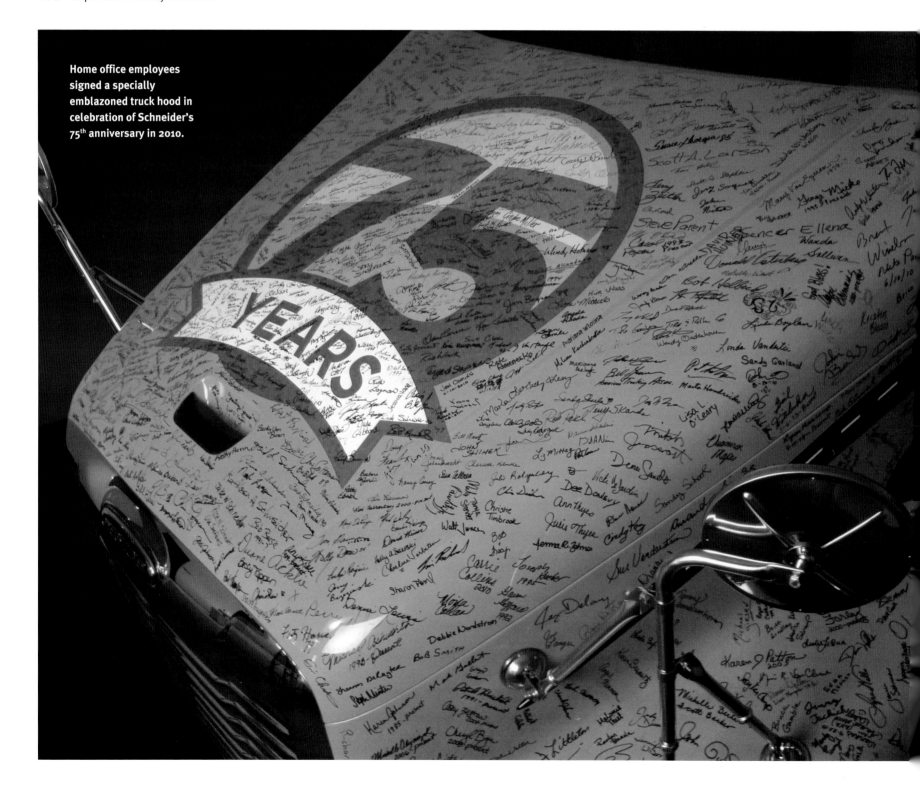

Home office employees signed a specially emblazoned truck hood in celebration of Schneider's 75th anniversary in 2010.

diversification of Schneider's leadership is evident in the fact that 40 percent of the members of today's executive team are women. While perhaps standard fare at other companies, the team's evolution is noteworthy in the histories of both Schneider and the overall transportation sector, long regarded as a male-dominated industry.

Continual reinvention and a fearless pursuit of the elusive goal called "excellence" were the hallmarks of Schneider during the first decade of the new century. Says Matheys: "During the greatest economic crisis since Al Schneider started the company, we were willing to change everything about the business except our core values." The capacity to evolve successfully is clearly one of those values.

AWARD-WINNING SERVICE

In 2010, Schneider National enjoyed its most award-winning year ever, garnering 43 honors from shippers, governmental organizations and industry media for a host of achievements in customer service, solutions and commitment to the environment. The Truckload Carriers Association (TCA) named Schneider a "Best Fleet to Drive For," reflecting the overall effectiveness of the company's driver programs. It was appropriate, then, that in June of that year, when the company celebrated its 75th anniversary, Lofgren spoke to Schneider associates while surrounded by members of the Million Mile Club, Schneider drivers who have completed at least a million miles on the road without an accident.

"The fact that we can stand here today and celebrate our 75th anniversary is a great testament to Al, Don and three generations of the Schneider family," Lofgren said. "The Schneider family, along with tens of thousands of Schneider associates, has been committed to the ideals this company has held dear for 75 years: safety, integrity, respect and excellence. Those values bond our company as strongly today as they did in 1935."

CARRYING THE FLAME

Some things are immutable. Others, like the company's old South Broadway offices, eventually outlive their time. That December, after almost 40 years, the complex, thick with memories, closed, but the company rolled on. By 2011, having completed the Intermodal conversion and well underway with the transformation of its enterprisewide information technology system while shrugging off the recession, Schneider was placing 1,600 loads on rails every day and was purchasing $1.7 billion in third-party transportation annually from more than 8,600 carriers.

In steady, dependable hands, the company seemed in all respects unstoppable when, on Friday, January 13, 2012, Don Schneider's courageous battle with Alzheimer's came to an end. His influence, most assuredly, did not. At his funeral five days later, Don's children remembered what he had meant to them.

"My father believed that the ability to endure pain made you a stronger person," said Tom. "He was competitive and full of passion. He worked the hardest, loved the deepest and gave 100 percent in everything he did."

"Dad was a strong advocate of self-confidence,"

A quintet of veteran drivers who became ambassadors for the company at its headquarters when their driving days were done participated in 75th anniversary festivities in June 2010. Left to right, Vern Johnson, who worked 38 years for the company; Bernie Watzka (52 years); Merlin Lardinois (55 years); Duane Livermore (58 years); and Julius Borley (64 years). Unavailable for the photo was Roger Klein (43 years).

Hundreds of Schneider associates, customers and community members attended a Celebration of Life event for Don Schneider at St. Norbert College following his death in 2012. Mary Gronnert, above, Don's executive assistant for more than 30 years and coordinator of the Schneider Foundation, was among the speakers who remembered Don with grace, warmth and humor. Attendees, right, included: front row, right to left, Bill Graves, president and CEO of the American Trucking Associations; Irwin Jacobs, founding chairman and CEO emeritus of Qualcomm, Inc.; and Steve Harmon, Kimberly-Clark's vice president of corporate transportation. Second row, right to left, Judy Lemke, Schneider's chief information officer; Lori Lutey, Schneider's chief financial officer; and Mark Rourke, president of Schneider Truckload Services.

added daughter Therese. "'Work is more than making money,' he said in an interview. 'It's about self-esteem, and everyone needs that.'"

Don was a humble man of faith whose heart was "filled with generosity and grounded in humility," remembered Kathleen, who recalled her dad saying, "My job is important, but it's no more important than the driver or the people in the service center."

It was a picture of Don echoed by her sister, Mary, whose recitation of the enduring lessons her father taught her included "Hug everyone as hard as you can," "Shake people's hands hard enough that they will never forget you" and "Be excellent in everything you do."

Son Paul remembered that, as his father sank into the twilight of Alzheimer's, he would often repeat questions again and again, unable to remember that he had asked them only moments before. Don's questions, said Paul, "spoke to how he was wired, what was important to him — health, education, family, God, and using one's God-given talents to be the best."

Don's last question was always, "'Are we beating J. B. Hunt?'" Paul recalled. "Dad was a fierce competitor. He would say, 'If you want to be the best, you need to beat the best.'"

A month after Don's death, on Wednesday, February 15, 2012, a celebration of his life was held at St. Norbert College, Don's alma mater in De Pere, Wisconsin. Hundreds of Schneider associates and customers attended — or watched as it was broadcast to many remote locations — to remember what a life it had been. Forged in the crucible of his father's hard discipline, his imprint upon the company, the industry and the community

The message was simple—"Let's Deliver"—as Schneider transformed the lobby of its corporate headquarters in early 2014 to capture associates' pride and passion for the company, the customers they serve and the quality of life they enhance every day. Outside the company's new Haul of Fame, below, one of those associates, Bob Wyatt, celebrated 40 consecutive years and four million miles of safe driving.

was huge, and St. Norbert's was among the greatest beneficiaries of his generosity. In 2008, Don's family had provided the lead gift for the St. Norbert College athletic complex, which was named the Donald J. Schneider Outdoor Complex in his honor; two years after Don's death, Pat Schneider donated $7 million to establish the Donald J. Schneider School of Business and Economics at St. Norbert.

Friends, colleagues, industry leaders and family members offered eulogies to Don and his extraordinary legacy. Even as they spoke, orange trucks were on the move, "beating the best," logging nearly three billion miles a year. The company that Al had launched and upon which Don had wielded such a transformative influence was metamorphosing yet again.

Always striving for the summit of success, Schneider's big orange trucks are a constant presence on America's highways, from sea to shining sea and everywhere in between.

BUILT TO LAST

As William B. Cassidy observed in that week's issue of *The Journal of Commerce*, the companies that survive for three-quarters of a century are those that consistently demonstrate a capacity to evolve. Al had laid the groundwork when he sold the family Plymouth, bought his first truck, purchased a down-and-out company and parlayed it into the precursor of Schneider National. Don and his team shifted direction when the industry was threatened by petroleum embargoes and rising fuel costs. They did it again in the volatile years after deregulation and again following the Great Recession of 2008. Schneider National continues to evolve, wrote Cassidy, "blazing a trail toward the future by redefining itself as an intermodal, short-haul truckload carrier with a strong emphasis on logistics and specialized transportation."

Indeed, though Don and Al Schneider are gone, the transformation they began is delivering results, and the torch has been passed to the next generation of men and women who are, most literally, driving their company, their name and everything they stood for into the future — with Don's determined yet now invisible hand still on the throttle of the company's governance. And, as if in tribute to the durable foundation that Al, Don and the Schneider family laid in 67 years of family management, the company turned in two of its most profitable years ever in 2012 and 2013.

"Al and Don taught us how to come through hard times when others fall by the wayside," says Lofgren. "Don took what his father had created, turned it into something beyond what Al could have imagined, and had the foresight to position it to flourish long after his days and under the leadership of future generations. He knew we would carry forward the family's vision, values and the dream of a company that is built to last."

Acknowledgments

Though I was denied the opportunity of interviewing either Al or Don Schneider as I researched this book, many people who knew and worked with them were willing to talk with me and share their memories. I was extremely fortunate to have been able to explore the past with Julius Borley, Vern Johnson, Roger Klein, Merlin Lardinois, Duane Livermore and Bernie Watzka, who drove Schneider trucks while the company was still young.

Members of the Schneider family who contributed their time and thoughts included Mrs. Pat Schneider, Don's wife; her sons, Tom and Paul J.; and Al's sons, David, Paul C., Jim and John. Paul C. Schneider was especially helpful, speaking with me on three occasions, and responding to many e-mailed questions. Unfortunately, due to his illness, I was unable to interview Donald J. Schneider, whose insights would have significantly enriched this book.

The list of other Schneider associates, current and former, who generously gave me their time is so long that, despite my best efforts to remember everyone, it is quite possible I overlooked someone. If so, please know that no slight is intended. I am deeply grateful to the following: Wayne Baudhuin, Larry Chaplin, Audrey Clancy, Pat Costello, Barbara DeJardin, Don Detampel, Steve Duley, Tom Gannon, Sheri Gerondale, Heather Green, Mary Gronnert, Todd Jadin, Donald Jauquet, Kathy Jerry, Kurt Koeppel, Gary Lautenslager, Judy Lemke, Chris Lofgren, Wayne Lubner, Bill Matheson, Paul McCarthy, John Miller, Don Osterberg, Steve Parent, Dan Pierce, Nancy and Glenn Remington, Woody Richardson, Dick Ritchie, Mark Rourke, Dick Schluttenhofer, Nicole Schoenborn, Larry Sur, Ed Thompson, Thomas Vandenberg and Mike Weiss.

Bob Harlan of the Green Bay Packers, Steve Harmon of Kimberly-Clark, Michelle Livingstone of The Home Depot, Matt Rose of Burlington Northern Santa Fe, John Swanson of the Kellogg School at Northwestern University, and Ernie Micek, founding member of the company's board of directors, all shared their experiences of working with Don Schneider. Jeanette Jacqmin of the Brown County Library and Christine Dunbar of the Brown County Historical Society helped me track down resources that gave me insight into what Green Bay was like when Al Schneider launched his business in the mid-1930s.

Lastly, my heartfelt gratitude to the Schneider steering committee—Todd Jadin, Steve Matheys, LuEllen Oskey, Mike Norder, Tom Vandenberg and, especially, Janet Bonkowski— for allowing me the privilege of telling this remarkable story. Without their help, writing this book would have been near impossible.

—Jim H. Smith

Timeline

1907
Aloysius J. "Al" Schneider is born to Jacob and Anna (Mannenbach) Schneider on March 16 in Johnsburg, Wisconsin.

1916
Having completed third grade, Al Schneider leaves school and begins working to enhance his family's income.

1933
Al Schneider moves to Green Bay and finds work driving a taxicab.

1934
Al transitions from cab driver to truck driver.

On June 5, at St. Peter Church in Johnsburg, he marries Agnes Halfmann.

1935
Al Schneider sells his car and uses the proceeds to buy his first truck, a used, two-and-a-half-ton International B. He lands steady work driving for Jules Peters Transfer.

Congress passes the Motor Carrier Act, amending the Interstate Commerce Act of 1887 and imposing national regulations on trucking companies.

Al and Agnes Schneider's first son, Donald, is born on October 19.

1936
Al joins Bur Wholesale Company, hauling beer from Milwaukee to Green Bay.

1937
Al and Agnes Schneider's second son, David, is born on January 1.

1938
Al, now driving for Olson Transport, purchases a second truck and adopts the business name A. J. Schneider and Sons.

Al leases his trucks to Green Bay moving and storage company Bins Transport. When Bins fails, he purchases the business and incorporates it as Schneider Transport & Storage, moving to Jackson Street in Green Bay.

1939
Al and Agnes Schneider's third son, Paul, is born on November 29.

1941
The International Brotherhood of Teamsters (IBT) unionizes Schneider Transport.

1944
Closing his independent storage business, Al purchases Allied Van Lines' agency Peters Transfer. Allied requires that Schneider's trucks be painted with the orange and black color scheme that later becomes Schneider's brand.

Schneider moves from Jackson Street to McDonald Street.

1946
Al and Agnes Schneider's fourth son, James, is born on June 4.

1948
Al and Agnes Schneider's fifth son, John, is born on November 17.

1950
The Teamsters' Central States Health and Welfare Fund is introduced. All unionized companies in the region are obliged to contribute to it.

1951
Al and Agnes Schneider's daughter, Kathleen, is born on September 15.

1954
David Schneider begins working for his father full time.

1955
The IBT introduces the Central States Pension Fund.

1956
Construction begins on the Interstate Highway System.

1957
Don Schneider graduates from St. Norbert College and, on June 15, marries Patricia "Pat" O'Brien. He drives a truck for Schneider Transport all summer and then, in September, leaves for a 13-month tour of duty with the Army in South Korea.

1958
Schneider Transport obtains its first interstate authority from the ICC and in the late summer, Julius Borley and Emil "Budd" Elm drive the first load of freight for Procter & Gamble across state lines.

1959
Don Schneider obtains his MBA from the University of Pennsylvania's Wharton School of Business and briefly contemplates embarking upon an East Coast career.

1960
Al asks Don to help run Schneider Transport, and Don and Pat return to Green Bay.

1961
Don Schneider is named general manager of Schneider Transport.

1962
Paul Schneider, Al's son, joins the company as operations manager.

1963
David Schneider leaves Schneider Transport and starts his own trucking company.

Schneider Transport purchases Green Bay–based Packer City Transit.

1964
On January 15, the trucking industry agrees to the first National Master Freight Agreement (NMFA) with the Teamsters.

1965
James "Jim" Schneider graduates from high school and enlists in the Army.

1966
Schneider takes over Weyerhauser's fleet in Marshfield, Wisconsin.

Paul Schneider is appointed Schneider Transport's director of safety, driver personnel and industrial relations.

1967
After completing his military service, Jim Schneider enrolls at the University of Wisconsin–Green Bay and joins Schneider Transport as a truck driver.

1968
Beginning a period of significant growth, Schneider acquires two companies and their transport authorities: Garrison Transport and Kampo Transit. Kampo is renamed Schneider Tank Lines.

Schneider Transport has authority to operate in all 48 contiguous United States.

1970
John Schneider graduates from the University of Wisconsin and works for Schneider briefly. Not interested in the trucking business, he moves to California to earn a PhD in clinical psychology and establishes a practice there.

Paul Schneider takes over management of Schneider Tank Lines.

Schneider Transport acquires Green Bay–based Lavery Transport.

1971
Schneider Transport moves to 2661 South Broadway in Green Bay.

Schneider Transport is granted authority to haul anything related to paper manufacturing to 11 states.

Schneider acquires its first computer, an NCR. The company develops its first electronic data management system, the Computer Assisted Real Time General Operations System (CARGOS).

Schneider Transport takes over Green Bay Packaging's fleet.

1972
Schneider acquires TransNational Truck of Amarillo, Texas.

1973
The Organization of Arab Petroleum Exporting Countries (OPEC) embargoes the United States. A nationwide, 55-mile-per-hour speed limit is imposed.

1974
Schneider acquires National Refrigerated Transport, Inc. of Tulsa, Oklahoma.

1975
Schneider introduces online billing.

1976
With the Teamsters' National Master Freight Agreement up for renewal, the union mounts a three-day national strike, obliging Schneider Transport to agree to abide by the NMFA.

Schneider agrees with the Teamsters on a percentage method of payment. Some drivers are upset, and 12 Green Bay drivers lead a five-day wildcat strike.

In August, Schneider employs 1,000 drivers for the first time.

Schneider Tank Lines abandons bulk milk transport and concentrates on chemicals. Paul Schneider creates National Bulk Transport.

1977
Schneider replaces its NCR computer and begins development of the $1 million Schneider Online Utilization Resource (SOURCE) platform. SOURCE goes online two years later.

Schneider purchases Green Bay–based Christensen Oil. Later, the company opens its first bulk fuel site at the Wise Garage in Dayton, Ohio, initiating the Schneider National Fuel System.

Schneider consolidates its nonunion subsidiaries under a holding company, American National Corporation (AMNACO).

1978
Schneider Transport achieves $100 million in annual revenues for the first time.

The company relocates administrative offices to 3061 and 3051 South Ridge Road in Green Bay.

OPEC embargoes the U.S. again. Schneider establishes the Schneider Fuel School and mounts a national campaign to teach its 2,000 drivers to conserve fuel by driving 55 miles per hour.

Anticipating deregulation of the trucking industry, Don Schneider and his management team develop a survival plan calling for withdrawal from the NMFA.

1979
The Teamsters call a 10-day strike on a number of carriers, including Schneider Transport.

Some Schneider drivers stage a 10-day wildcat strike against Schneider.

1980
President Jimmy Carter signs the Motor Carrier Act of 1980, deregulating the trucking industry.

Schneider's information technology team installs a private branch exchange (PBX) telephone system, dramatically improving telecommunications for customers and drivers alike. Schneider buys high WATS line capacity, enabling creation of the New Improved Telephone Resource Operation (NITRO), with which drivers can directly call Schneider operators.

1982
AMNACO becomes Schneider National, Inc.

Jim Schneider launches American Pacific Express, Inc.

Schneider opens its first driver training center.

Annual revenue reaches $200 million.

Schneider engineers adapt 3M's mainframe software to create the world's first load control center.

Schneider moves its headquarters to a 102,000-square-foot building at 2777 Ridge Rd.

Schneider exits the NMFA and negotiates an individual labor agreement with the Teamsters. The majority of Schneider drivers approve the new labor agreement, which allows Teamsters' drivers to keep their jobs and benefits.

The company uses its large WATS line capacity to establish Applied Communications Systems, which will become Schneider Communications.

Jim Schneider sells American Pacific Express to Schneider National in return for stock. He remains in charge of the business, which operates out of the old McDonald Street facility.

Schneider posts record-breaking sales of $300 million.

The last union work stoppage against Schneider takes place, against Schneider Tank Lines.

1983
Al Schneider dies on March 3.

1984
Don Schneider recapitalizes the company.

Schneider acquires International Transport, the nation's largest heavy-load transport operation.

Schneider begins using Micro Dispatch Aids, software that analyzes cost and location to recommend load assignments.

Schneider creates the Special Services Division (SSD), a separate Schneider Transport bargaining unit. New drivers hired to work in the SSD are covered by its contract, not the Central States plans.

1985
American Pacific Express is renamed APX.

Schneider National Carriers is formed, embracing all of Schneider's nonunion entities. Schneider stops hiring in the SSD and accelerates hiring in Schneider National.

Schneider adds 17 truck stops to the Schneider National Fuel Network.

The Million Mile Club, comprising drivers who've completed at least a million consecutive miles without an accident, is introduced to celebrate their accomplishments and Schneider's safety culture.

1986
All of Schneider's 2,700 trucks are retrofitted with Tripmaster fuel monitoring technology.

Don Schneider creates a board of directors for Schneider National.

Schneider's first company-owned remote operating center opens in Seville, Ohio.

1988
Don Schneider signs a $20 million contract with Qualcomm to adapt OmniTRACS, a satellite-supported tracking and messaging service, for the entire Schneider fleet.

1989
Schneider National becomes an international business, obtaining authority to haul in Quebec, Ontario and British Columbia.

1990
Schneider International Transport completes a multimillion-dollar modernization of its fleet and is rebranded as Schneider Specialized Carriers.

1991
SensorTRACS automates remote collection of fuel utilization data.

Schneider goes intermodal with an agreement with the Southern Pacific Railroad and names the operation TruckRail.

1992
Schneider achieves $1 billion in revenues for the first time.

Schneider signs TruckRail agreements with 10 more major railroads.

Schneider opens a new, $15 million, 220,000-square-foot customer service and corporate business center in the Green Bay suburb of Ashwaubenon.

1993
Schneider Logistics, Inc. is introduced.

1994
Schneider Logistics lands the largest logistics contract ever awarded, to manage shipment of all 435,000 General Motors parts every day.

In the company's largest private fleet conversion ever, Schneider Dedicated takes over Kimberly-Clark's fleet. Scott Paper soon inks a similar distribution/logistics deal with Schneider.

Schneider begins operations in Mexico.

Wired magazine profiles Schneider National as "an information system masquerading as a trucking line."

1995
Agnes Schneider passes away after a long battle with Alzheimer's disease.

Schneider Communications is sold to the Frontier Communications Corporation.

Schneider surpasses the $2 billion mark.

Schneider Dedicated converts Anchor Foods' Anchor Express fleet.

The Teamsters begin expelling Schneider drivers from the union's pension and health funds.

1997
Schneider's first Web application allows customers to check the location and status of freight online around the clock.

2002
Don Schneider steps down in the summer, and Christopher B. Lofgren is named president and CEO. Lofgren begins a customer-centric re-engineering of Schneider's core business practices.

2004
Schneider completes its decade-long endeavor to manage millions of dollars in withdrawal liability penalties incurred when the Teamsters expelled Schneider drivers from union pension and health plans.

2005
Schneider surpasses $3 billion in annual revenues.

2006
Acquiring American Overseas Air Freight, Schneider becomes the first truckload carrier to offer door-to-door international logistics services.

Schneider Logistics opens an office in Shanghai, China.

2007
Granted authority to operate as a domestic carrier and logistics services provider in China, Schneider acquires the operating assets of Bayoun Logistics, one of China's top 30 private logistics enterprises.

Schneider's Mexico Express Intermodal service offers unprecedented access to Mexico's prime industrial center, boosting capacity, expediting customs clearance and enhancing freight security for cross-border shipments.

Don Schneider resigns from the board of directors.

Schneider hires Oracle to create a powerful new information platform for the company, beginning a significant, seven-year technology transformation called Quest.

2008
Responding to booming Asian imports and tightening rail capacity, Intermodal initiates a sweeping "overnight" conversion of its cargo containers to double-stack models.

2010
Schneider celebrates its 75th anniversary.

The Million Mile Club boasts more than 2,200 members.

Schneider National experiences its most award-winning year ever.

2012
Don Schneider dies on Friday, January 13. An event celebrating his life is held, taking place at the same time as the company is substantially transforming its business.

2013
Schneider completes Quest, the largest technology implementation in its history.

Index